Bridezilla: True Tales from Etiquette Hell

First Printing 2002

Cover and Book Design by Ryan Myers

Illustration by Kevin Middleton

ISBN 0-9663870-4-X

Library of Congress Catalog Number: 2002 103262

Printed in the United States of America by
Ginny's Printing and Copying
1501-B West Anderson Lane, Austin, Texas 78757

Published by
Salado Press
P. O. Box 719
Salado, Texas 76571

CONTENTS

FOREWORD
by David Feldman vii

PROLOGUE ix

CHAPTER 1:
Welcome to the Wonderful World of Bridezilla! 1

CHAPTER 2:
It All Starts With the Ring 13

CHAPTER 3:
It's the Little Things That Mean a Lot 31

CHAPTER 4:
Shower Me With Gifts or I Will Destroy Tokyo 51

CHAPTER 5:
Meddle Not In the Affairs of Bridezilla
for You Are Crunchy and Good With Ketchup 77

CHAPTER 6:
"I Am Queen Bridezilla and I Rule the Earth!"
Extreme Bridezillas 97

CHAPTER 7:
Groomonsters and Other Freaks of Nature 123

CHAPTER 8:
You Should Thank Me for Not Destroying Tokyo! 141

EPILOGUE 153

ABOUT THE AUTHORS 158

SELECTED BIBLIOGRAPHY 160

ACKNOWLEDGEMENTS 161

FOREWORD

They may look like you and me. They walk among us, undetected. But just as atomic bomb testing reawakened the prehistoric reptile, Godzilla, nuptials can unleash monsters smaller in stature but far more terrifying than any overgrown lizard: Bridezillas!

Until I read this book, I was blithely unaware of this danger to our way of life. But Noe Spaemme and Jeanne Hamilton have bravely gone where no researcher has dared go before, and catalogued the many species of Bridezillas, and their occasional soul mates, Groomonsters. You need this book to protect yourself from this burgeoning scourge upon the sea of matrimony; after all, a Bridezilla might invite you to her wedding, or even worse, ask you to be one of her attendants. Even the bride of Frankenstein was kind enough not to demand a lavish shower from her attendants, or festoon her bridesmaids' dresses with butt bows the size of Latvia.

To you who are contemplating marriage, or love someone who is, I offer humble advice: Please read this book, or give this book to the bride-to-be. Just as a previously unimpeachable lizard was mutated by the effects of radioactivity (Godzilla had no prior rap sheet), so the occasional otherwise lovely human being can turn a shower, a bachelorette party, or even the wedding itself into a living Hell on Earth, while justifying her misbehavior by screeching the four most dreaded words in the English language: "It's my special day!"

Scariest of all, you might one day look into the mirror and see a Bridezilla peering back at you. While no vaccine has yet been invented to eradicate rampant wedding misbehavior from the world, <u>Bridezilla: True Tales from Etiquette Hell</u> is the only known antidote.

- David Feldman

Author of the Imponderables® series of books and popular culture writer

New York, 2002

PROLOGUE

"Hmm, they sound like candidates for Etiquette Hell."
alt.wedding, June 1996

Thus the concept of an Etiquette Hell for greedy, bratty brides was started as a joke on the alt.wedding and soc.couples.wedding Usenet newsgroups over six years ago. The idea eventually materialized as a real Web page in the spring of 1997. Since its creation five years ago, thousands of true stories have been submitted to www.etiquettehell.com by visitors who yearned for a place to vent their frustrations about their treatment at the hands of Bridezillas, Wicked Witches, Groomonsters, rogue bridesmaids, nefarious vendors, and tacky guests. These victims of inflicted etiquette faux pas gain some validation for their feelings of being used and abused by casting their antagonist into the bowels of Etiquette Hell and then enjoying the entertainment value these antics deserving of Hell give other readers of the site.

A wedding can bring out the best in a person but often brings out the worst. A bride, in particular, seems most susceptible to mutating into a beast no family member or friend can recognize because a magical ring was placed on the third finger of her left hand. The growing popularity of the www.etiquettehell.com Web site parallels the increase in tantrums and other incidents of rude, selfish behavior by brides in American culture. The word

"Bridezilla" is so new it cannot be found in any dictionary, yet an Internet search for the word finds its usage well-established. By definition, a Bridezilla describes a subspecies of a bride-to-be who believes her wedding day is "her day," that she is princess for the day, that the world owes her, and that her every desire and whim for the "perfect wedding" is to be catered to instantly and subserviently by friends, family, and vendors under threat of thermonuclear meltdown.

A much lesser-known variant of the Bridezilla is her mate, the Groomonster, who is known for exerting his will on unsuspecting friends and family. While writing a book focused almost entirely on Bridezillas might smack of sexism, the awful truth is that ninety-eight percent of all stories submitted to Etiquette Hell detail the excruciatingly tasteless behavior of women who have succumbed to the temptation of being a Bridezilla.

This book defines and explains how to avoid Bridezilla behavior, relates true stories of Bridezillas, and offers practical advice on dealing with a full-blown case of Bridezillaism in your loved one. While the Web site, www.etiquettehell.com, is a place where victims of Bridezillas can vent their frustrations, this book is meant to be tongue-in-cheek, yet informative, in addressing the trend of Bridezilla behavior. Some etiquette blunders are so deliberate and so egregious the only response is to laugh lest one dissolve into tears of woe. Whether you are selecting this book for yourself or as a gift for your favorite Bridezilla, this book is perfect for any prospective bride and groom about to face the temptation of becoming Bridezilla and Groomonster during the wedding planning process.

If you have a true story of a Bridezilla or any other wedding faux pas so heinous you just have to nominate the offender for inclusion in Etiquette Hell, direct your browser to:

www.etiquettehell.com

and submit your story via the links provided.

1) WELCOME TO THE WONDERFUL WORLD OF THE BRIDEZILLA!

A Short Descent From Mother's Daughter to the Creature From Hell

CHAPTER ONE

Bridezilla. What a horrid creature a bride must be—radiant in glory, dressed in white, and veiled in modesty—for her to be given such an awful name, full of mental imagery worthy of a bad Hollywood "B" flick.

And horrid she is! She is greedy, pouty, loud, rude, selfish, immature, obnoxious, unreasonable, irrational, spiteful—in short, hardly worthy of the platitude normally given to a bride. And those are some of her better qualities. But how did the Bridezilla come to be such a common fixture in our modern culture?

To be sure, it was unseemly during the Victorian era for any bride to appear to be anything less than demure and acquiescent. This was, after all, the era of outward demonstrations of one's piety and purity and a denouncement of self-indulgence—at least publicly. We know full well that the public display was quite often very different from how one really lived. The planning of the wedding was not primarily the task of the bride but that of her family, chiefly her mother. In the absence of a mother, then an aunt or grandmother took on the task. If the bride was an orphan and still in someone's charge, then her sponsors acted on her behalf. The Victorian bride followed all the rules of social decorum to a fault; otherwise her reputation suffered as did that of her family and her new husband. Yes, even people in the Victorian era loved to gossip. It was important during this era that one aim for the aristocracy of character rather than of position. By attaining the status of a person of good moral and sensible character, then one also likely achieved a noted social position. For a time, one could not be thought of highly in social circles if one was of poor character.

This is not to say that hints of Bridezillaism were absent during the wedding planning season. Those newspaper writers who related the comings and goings of those in the social scene were quick to note items such as the dress worn or the lavish decorations, adding a hint of elegant mystery by writing, "The couple left the following afternoon for their secret honeymoon destination." Such reports certainly inflamed the desires of pious young women who silently dreamed of their wedding day, when they too could wear the orange blossoms of purity and the white dress of joy (and of serious social significance) and be whisked away to a secret honeymoon location. When at last her prince had come, true emotions often surfaced, and the demure and oh-so-proper young lady used her well-honed charms to get her way—a formal church wedding with the most lavish floral decorations available. In the case where the bride was not so inclined to seek the wedding of her dreams, it was not unusual for her mother (in particular the nouveau riche or society climbers) to press for the finest things possible despite the etiquette writers' mandate of restraint. Never mind that etiquette of the day still pressed for simplicity and understated elegance. In other words, putting on a show for the neighbors (or keeping up with the Tudors) was considered the poorest of taste, which reflected very badly on the husband. True, there were rules about the treatment of a formal wedding, but much was expected of the bride and her family in return for the show of such regalia. The more showy the wedding, the deeper the social obligations.

Conversely, those who did not want a great fuss or did not have the means to host a lavish affair simply married in their Sunday best, at home, with immediate family and perhaps a few friends.

Toward the end of the Victorian era, as World War I came to an end, Americans were in for a major social revolution. Many of those who survived the Great War were in no mood for restraint and decorum. The flapper era of the Roaring '20s saw a more persistent cheekiness and social decadence in all factors of life, including weddings. Movies, magazines, and books were now preaching a new boldness. While it was still unseemly for nice girls from good families to put on garish displays or behave with impunity, that didn't stop them from wanting more and following the examples set in the media instead of the ones given from the pulpit or in private by their mothers. Nice girls learned more in the flickering darkness of the theater from silent films such as "The Matrimaniac" and "The Probation Wife" than mothers and fathers would have wanted.

Once the country moved out of the Great Depression—even though a sense of frugality still hung in the air—a wedding was a grand thing to celebrate, and in style. Those who made it through the darkness of a broken economy were now able to spend a little on themselves or their families. Fathers who were once eager to relinquish that extra mouth to someone who could afford to feed her were now holding on to their little girls a little longer. The young man who would claim Daddy's little girl had better be good enough for her. Once so proven, Daddy was ready to do that which would please his girl and reflect favorably upon his family. Fathers who did not care for the suitor or did not approve of the marriage, for whatever reason, often just fell out of the picture while the mother took over. During this time, media continued to play an important role in the development of impressionable young minds. Films like "Gone With the Wind" and "Jezebel" showed us how much fun it could be to be a little wicked. The dresses were pretty, there was money (sometimes), the men were dashing, and it was an era of cinematic romance. Modern movies were no better; "Dodsworth," "The Gay Bride," "Hired Wife," "Wedding Present," and others portrayed brides as cunning and bold, more so than most people really were. But the influence of the media was strong, and soon life began to imitate art. The real Bridezilla was just around the corner, lurking, waiting for just the right moment to pounce on the unsuspecting.

Compounding the effect of films on the public were ladies' magazines, Hollywood tattletale magazines, "confession" magazines, and, on the heels of those, comic books. *True Bride-to-Be Romances, Young Brides, Wedding Bells, Love and Marriage, Bride's Romances, Young Romance, Heart Throbs, Romantic Marriage,* and *My Secret Marriage* were just some of the comic books produced in the 1950s.

The movies, magazines, and comics exploded, carried along by the post-war boom. Women who were once completely in the charge of men were now able to prove their own merit in the world, having carried much of the American home war effort

5

themselves, without men at home. The time, days, and age when it would be unthinkable for a woman not to be completely demurred to a man were over. Women would never again be chattel. Although it was still something of a shock to the culture at large, it was fact that some women who had previously worked "for the cause" now worked because they enjoyed it. Woman was her own person. Naturally, some worked out of necessity, but no longer could it be assumed that a woman in the workplace was there because of some family misfortune. Young women were more able to make choices of their own without worrying about what their parents would think. Of course, the well-bred young woman still lived according to her life's station and followed all the proper rules of decorum.

Bridezilla looms. Now the country had women who worked because they wanted to; they went to college to earn a B.A., B.S., or Ph.D—not necessarily an M.R.S. Women were making choices. And thanks to the aforementioned media, women had even more choices put before them. They could choose to do what they saw on the silver screen and in magazines. They could choose to follow a screen idol and have a wedding beyond their means. They could be influenced by fabulous weddings such as those of Elizabeth to Philip, Grace to Ranier, Liz to everybody, Rita to Aly, and so on.

To be sure, film has always had an impact on trends and what people come to accept as normal. There is, after all, the notion that art imitates life. However, more often than not, life imitates art when setting new trends.

Through television and especially film, unsuspecting women have been introduced to fantasy thinly disguised as fiction and supposedly based, in some aspect, on reality. The creators of these fantasies are so very skilled in their craft that the viewer comes to believe that the fantasy surely is reality somewhere, and if it is reality somewhere then why not right here!

Naturally, those in the retail business are very eager to cater to the fantasy; it is a very lucrative business. One source puts the bridal business at $32 BILLION annually in the United States alone. With some 2.4 million couples walking down the aisle each year, that's an allotment of $19,000 per wedding. Of course, when we factor in those who elope, those who have simple civil ceremonies, and those who pull off a perfectly proper and marvelous wedding for under $19,000, that means a lot of brides are spending well over the benchmark. However, one does not need a lot of money to be a Bridezilla. Boorish behavior crosses all monetary class lines.

Helping the billion-dollar bridal business and spreading the notion of Bridezillaism are bridal and wedding magazines and Web sites. "It's YOUR day!!" they all proclaim in bold graphics. "Do it YOUR way!" they admonish. They might toss in a little gratuitous etiquette help, most of which is more helpful to the bridal business than to the bride. Go ahead and put registry cards in your wedding invitations; your guests will thank you for it, they advise. Sure, it's okay for your mother to host your shower in her home, they coo. But they give dire warnings about not having enough pâté or custom-labeled wine as if either were as necessary as the marriage license. Pish posh!

With more and more couples living together prior to marriage, we must also hold the Groomonster somewhat accountable for putting the Bridezilla on her pedestal. Not willing to incur the wrath of a hormonal, overexcited, highly emotional thing that shares the bed, he tries to stop all wars and calm the bride by saying, "Whatever you want to do, honey... I'm in agreement. After all, it's your day—you should have whatever you want." AGH! While this will make him a god in her eyes—if only for the moment—it won't make the Bridezilla any more tame, and it is likely to reinforce the notion that Bridezillaism is A-OK. After all, the Groomonster, the love of the Bridezilla's life, is in agreement. Never mind that he probably has no idea that he just agreed that the guests should buy tickets to the bar at the reception; he's going to get to the wedding in relative peace—and in one piece if he can help it.

Remember the post-Victorian mother who wanted her daughter to have all that she herself wasn't able to have? The Momzilla isn't gone. In fact, she is fully present and often works in tandem with the Bridezilla. She insists on hosting the bridal shower (one of twenty showers yet to come!). She insists that ALL of the out-of-town guests be invited to the rehearsal dinner, which the groom's parents are hosting. As a courtesy, she makes reservations for the out-of-towners at five-star hotels ("Nothing is too good for our guests!"), making certain, of course, she has obtained their credit card numbers prior to booking the rooms. She insists that black is the only suitable color for her matronly figure, and she must wear black or she will not attend. And she insists, more often than not, on going into debt so that her Baby Bridezilla can have whatever she wants.

How do we know this? Let's look at the statistics. In mid-2001, consumer indebtedness, not including mortgages, was at an all-time high of $1.58 TRILLION. You don't think the $32-billion wedding business is not a part of that, do you? And that's for products we know to be wedding-oriented; many goods and services provided at weddings don't necessarily come from the usual wedding vendors, and this figure does not include gifts or travel costs incurred by guests.

But even if Momzilla has a level head and holds her grown daughter responsible for her own wedding plans, brides are still apt to say "But I WANT it!" and go deeply into debt to have it. For one day. For one day, a Bridezilla is willing to put her marriage into serious debt. Truly one trademark of the Bridezilla: to have whatever she wants no matter what the cost.

The road to becoming a Bridezilla hasn't been a long one, historically speaking. And sadly, as a result of the "do it if it feels good" era of the 1960s, the Bridezilla is now far too common. What was once relegated to whispered gossip as if to discuss an overfilled sewer is now so common that we have more than enough material to fill volumes of true tales of the Bridezilla.

It is a sad commentary on society, but what the hell. Etiquette Hell, that is. They're here. They're staying. They're fodder for those who would never behave so poorly. Or would they? Step now, very carefully, into the archives of that very warm place, populated by all that embodies Bridezilla.

2) IT ALL STARTS WITH THE RING

CHAPTER TWO

He had planned this moment for weeks. The dinner at their special restaurant had been exceptionally delicious and memorable owing to the attentiveness of the professional wait-staff. The atmosphere was oh-so-romantic as the music played softly in the background and the stars twinkled. His eyes drank in her every move. She looked lovely in her pale blue silk dress that accentuated her cascading curls. He gasped inwardly and felt his heart leap into his throat as she looked up from her dessert to gaze at him with her deep brown eyes. Now was the right moment, right now. Slipping his hand into his pocket, he opened the ring box while mouthing the words that are known to dissolve intelligent women into incoherent puddles of tears: "Will you marry me?"

Little did he know that placing the diamond ring on his beloved's left hand would initiate a metamorphosis, as his future wife would rise from the primordial ooze of singlehood to evolve into a fire-breathing, Tokyo-destroying Bridezilla of epic proportions.

FIRST THE RING...

As a dozen of us sat there, waiting for dinner to begin, my friend lifted her glass and toasted herself and her boyfriend. "I just wanted to let you all know that Dave and I are getting engaged, just as soon as we have the ring. It's all picked out. It costs six THOUSAND dollars!"

Uh-oh, this is a bad warning sign of a nascent Bridezilla waiting to metastasize. The bride has placed a greater emphasis on the monetary value of the engagement ring than the symbolism it is supposed to represent. The bearer of this tale went on to relate that the groom looked like he wanted to crawl under the table and nearly called off the wedding after catching a glimpse of the potential Bridezilla he had asked to marry him. Subspecies of this type of Bridezilla are the ones who equate the value of the diamond with the value of the groom's love for her. Or who manipulatively whine that they can't possibly be engaged if they don't have a ring to show to everyone. A groom should consider himself lucky if his intended rears her ugly Bridezilla head early enough in the wedding planning process that preventative measures can be taken. Forewarned is forearmed!

My aunt told her kids when they were younger that they could have her mother's and grandmother's diamonds to give to their future brides when it was time to get engaged. They could have the diamonds set as they wished. Although the stones were not large, they weren't exactly chips, and the fact that these were family heirlooms might be considered an extra honor for some girls as entrance to the family.

My cousin and his long-time girlfriend took the largest diamond to a jeweler and designed a custom ring. When the ring was ready, my cousin gave it to his bride-to-be and announced their engagement to everyone.

A few weeks later, the bride whined to my cousin (after showing her new engagement ring to her friends and co-workers) that the diamond wasn't suitable and she wanted a bigger diamond! My doting cousin gave the ring back to his mother and took all his money from his savings and bought her a bigger diamond. His fiancée could now show off her "rock" to friends and co-workers.

Our Bridezilla obviously cares more about what others think about her beloved's symbol of intent to marry than the intent itself. Since the bride knew the size of the heirloom diamond and how the setting would look, she had no call to whine about a new ring. The prudent groom would have not kowtowed to this bride's whine; he would perhaps have suggested that they save up over the years for a special anniversary ring—assuming they could even make it to an anniversary!

THEN SETTING THE WEDDING DATE...

Shortly after my boyfriend proposed to me rather unexpectedly, my stepsister (who lived in another city) stopped talking to me. I eventually found out through a family member that she was LIVID that we were considering a date so close to hers. In fact, she and her fiancé refused to attend my wedding and she "uninvited" me as bridesmaid.

When I finally got her to talk to me again, she said that I was completely insensitive and a jerk for having the audacity to take away her spotlight, especially since I already did so once by getting engaged so soon after she did (as if my fiancé was supposed to consult with her fiancé on proposal timing!). She told me that it was obvious I knew nothing about proper etiquette, because everyone knew that there should be no weddings six months before hers or six months after hers!

It is the height of Bridezillaism to reign and rule over the calendar to make sure no one in the circle of family and friends gets married anywhere near the bride's chosen day. With this bride, it was not just her day; it was her year, with manipulative tantrums thrown in to enforce her rule. The real translation of "You are stealing my spotlight" is "Your wedding has the potential of not only being better than mine but also diminishing my amount of booty."

Another mark of Bridezillaism is suddenly to spew etiquette dictates of "everybody knows." Clearly, this Bridezilla didn't know, as there is no such "rule" about spacing between weddings. And it's always the Bridezilla who uses the excuse of "etiquette" to throw a tantrum, which is not at all proper.

The family received a wedding invitation from my cousin. We purchased a lovely gift from the registry and sent it to the bride's home. While confirming travel arrangements, the cousin called and left a message that we were uninvited to the wedding! About a month after the wedding, we received a thank-you letter for the gift; in it he detailed all the reasons why we were uninvited. But he kept the gift anyway.

While not as common as Bridezillas, Groomonsters do exist to wreak havoc on their guests and family. This Groomonster did the unthinkable and actually retracted an invitation already issued. There is no situation that justifies the retraction of even a single invitation once it has been issued.

The faux pas was compounded by his oversight in not returning the gift, resulting in a classic example of the presents being more important than the presence. And finally, his committing to paper a list of complaints toward another—worse still, a family member—showed a serious lack of good judgment. Whatever this Groomonster's reasons were for retracting the invitation, his subsequent actions were completely uncalled for.

My husband's friend from his hometown was getting married in February. She called to tell him about it and asked for our address so she could send an invitation. When we received it, we immediately RSVP'd "yes." A couple of weeks later, the bride left a message on our voice mail saying that her secretary at work had mistakenly mailed some invitations that were not supposed to be sent—like ours. Can you believe it?! We were uninvited by voice mail!

Once the invitation has been issued, even by accident, it cannot be retracted unless one wants to appear in Etiquette Hell as a prima facie example of a fire-breathing, knuckle-dragging clod. (Exception: ALL invitations are recalled in the event of cancellation or postponement of the wedding.) The best alternative is to suck it up, say nothing, and pay the extra money to include all the guests who were sent invitations. The worst alternative is to do what this bride did, which was to confirm in the guests' minds that indeed their possible inclusion at this wedding would have been as second-class guests.

My aunt recently attended a hastily organized wedding. The invitations had a notation of "greenback reception" (meaning: bring money not gifts) AND to bring a dish for the potluck meal!

The classic Bridezilla presumes that everyone owes her something on her wedding day, and requesting that guests not only fund her wedding but cater it as well ensures the Bridezilla of an especially warm spot in Etiquette Hell. It places beloved family and friends not in the role of honored guests but rather financial backers of the impending wedding. Guests should resist the urge to condone this greedy, grubby behavior with their participation. This faux pas is so serious that any wedding invitation that makes any notation of gifts, money, or "bring this or that" should be tossed into the shredder and not given another thought.

Because the bride and groom were planning to set up house in Switzerland, they included on the invitation a request that in lieu of gifts, people should wire money to their Swiss bank account. The bank name and account number were included on the invitation.

This is just an upscale version of begging, justified in the bride's and groom's minds that they are correct in their presumption that their friends and family not only owe them a wedding gift but also can be told what to give. Including bank account numbers, deposit slips, and bank telephone numbers in a wedding invitation conveys the message to one's most beloved friends and family that their presence—or even their simple blessing of the wedding—requires a financial donation to the engaged couple. The lowbrow versions of the Swiss bank account invitation are the "Wishing Well Wedding, $20 and up only" as well as the "Presentation" notation, which means that the bride and groom will sit upon their thrones while their subjects (the guests) present them with envelopes of cash. Sometimes the bride even carries a birdcage or satin purse throughout the reception to collect cash. All of these pay-ups are in addition to the wedding gift. Remember, do not feed the animals by rewarding this behavior. Refuse to participate in any wedding-related extortion scheme, no matter how well dressed the perpetrators.

Friends and family who want to bestow material blessings on the couple are more than welcome to, and it's their choice as to what form those material blessings will take. But there is no call for any bride or groom to assume that friends and family are required to do so, and there is never an occasion in which it is correct to make requests or demands for a specific type of gift.

My husband and I were recently invited to the wedding of one of his good college friends. In the invitation was a deposit slip to a bank because the couple were "...saving for a house."

We've included this particular true tale here, since many people are incredulous that someone would actually be so audaciously greedy as to insert a bank deposit slip into a wedding invitation. Such an invitation leaves a tainted, sour taste in the mouths of its recipients, who wonder if the wedding is merely a clever ruse to raise capital for real estate investments. Invitees are under no obligation to give money, and serious consideration should be employed in deciding whether to attend, since attendance may have the appearance of sanctioning greedy, inappropriate solicitations. If one wishes to accept this invitation, then consider an appropriate gift of a reference book, which deals with personal money management, since this couple appears to be clueless. Such a gift would be truly thoughtful and practical.

The bride had sent people invitations to her wedding—a very exclusive "high society" affair at a posh resort—with either "A" or "B" written on the invitation. Guests who received a "B" invitation would be allowed to attend in the event someone with an "A" invitation declined. In other words, "B" guests were on a stand-by list if "A" guests canceled or declined! I was astonished! The bride's explanation for this was written in the invitation: "I would love to have everyone present, but since this is just not possible, you will be notified if a space becomes available." The nerve!!

While some etiquette writers may view "A" and "B" guest lists

The invitation arrived three weeks before the wedding with an RSVP deadline long since passed. Apparently we not only did not make the "A" list but we didn't make the "B" list either.

as marginally acceptable, Miss Jeanne thinks they are social abominations that categorize supposedly close friends and family into hierarchies based on proximity and relationship. What they say is that the hosts of the wedding planned a wedding that exceeded their budget and that they placed a higher priority on meeting expensive tastes than on including alleged friends, such that only a limited number of guests could be invited. Pity the poor "friend" who discovers that a plate of prime rib at a posh resort was more important than the relationship!

However, Auntie Noe sees the "A" and "B" lists as a necessary evil when one simply has more friends than space or finances can comfortably accommodate. As long as "B" listers never ever find out they are "B" listers, then there is no harm. Even if one receives a late invitation to the wedding—or to any event—one is not to second-guess the host's motives, unless untoward motives have been made known, since an invitation to a social event is generally an honor in itself. There is a specific protocol to using "A" and "B" lists, and if it is properly followed no one is ever the wiser and it works to the benefit of all concerned.

This Bridezilla landed squarely in Etiquette Hell by using her wedding invitation to announce to the world that she "A" and "B" listed her guests, thereby making some feel oh so hoity-toity (for the moment) and the rest to wonder why they were not so special. Imagine the conversation at the reception: "Hello, I'm George Smith and this is my wife, Mary. We're 'A' listers. And you?" Of course, we'd toss George into Etiquette Hell as well for being so insensitive. But those who are not like George would surely feel uncomfortable knowing that they were "A" listed while others were "B" listed, thereby realizing that they too are subject to a pseudo class distinction in the minds of the hosts. One must never make any guest feel anything less than completely special.

A woman I worked with sent out this e-mail to all the company employees: "I'm getting married next month. The first ten people to reply are invited to attend my wedding ceremony."

This is an insulting invitation, because it presumes guests are like cattle that can be summoned to appear with the resulting first ten respondents "winning" the stampede to the wedding. Appropriately, the recipient of this e-mail invitation treated it with all the dignity it deserved and hit the delete key. The moral of the story is that invitations matter, because they are the first indication to guests of the type of wedding being planned.

It is proper to issue very informal invitations when the event itself is very informal. And some weddings are indeed incredibly casual. A telephoned invitation for a spur-of-the-moment wedding is just as proper as sending a fax when time is of the essence. But it is never correct to turn the guest list into a competition to see who can get there first. No matter how casual the event, guests should not be treated *that* casually.

BUYING THE WEDDING GOWN...

On my wedding day, I wore a beautiful replica of a French designer gown which was made and given to me by a close friend. My stepbrother's fiancée approached me near the end of the wedding. They were to be married a few weeks after we were. She told me that she had the same wedding dress as mine. I smiled and said, "Great minds think alike!" She wasn't happy and continued on, "No, you don't get it! I have that exact same dress for my wedding."

A few weeks later, we traveled to my stepbrother's wedding. I should have known to expect trouble because he told me that his fiancée was still pouting about our "matching" wedding dresses. At the reception dinner, my husband and I sat at a table with some of the older adults. After we chitchatted for a bit, I introduced myself and discovered our heretofore-delightful companions were the grandmother and aunt of the bride. The grandmother turned to the aunt and said quite loudly, "Oh, so SHE'S the one who ripped off my baby princess's dress."

Just as a bride cannot have an exclusive lock on wedding dates, it is unrealistic to expect everyone else marrying in the same year to have the psychic foresight to know which dress everyone has chosen to avoid duplication. This particular bride has the pitiable situation of being born into a family of Bridezillas and Bridezilla knock-offs who help reinforce the false notion that she is the "princess" and that she is justified in dissolving into a whiny mess over a dress.

Our hero bride could have responded to the grandmother with nothing more than a fit of hysterical laughter and made her point without resorting to any other comment.

THE "FAUX" WEDDING...

After college, Fiona moved out of state and we drifted apart. But when I received an invitation to her bridal shower in town, I eagerly accepted. When Fiona found out I too was engaged to be married, she asked me about my plans. I told her it was going fine but tending to so many details had us thinking about eloping. Leaning towards me, Fiona whispered conspiratorially, "Can you keep a secret?" Before I could even answer, she said she and her fiancé had eloped several months earlier but none of their friends or family knew. I was too stunned to say anything, but I didn't stay much longer at this "pretend" shower, and I declined to attend the so-called wedding.

Think of the trouble, cost, and vacation days everyone wasted attending Fiona's fairy-tale wedding!

The only reason for this Bridezilla's deception was a completely selfish motive not to be deprived of a big party and all the gifts associated with a large wedding event. The wickedness of this deceit is that it inconveniences guests into attending a sham wedding and leads the guests to believe they are witnessing a special event. When Etiquette Hell first debuted in 1997, "Faux Wedding" stories were unheard of, but in the last two years the numbers of submitted stories has grown exponentially. This growth can be attributed to a desire to "have it all," which means the financial benefits of marriage such as health insurance coverage, while also reaping the benefits of a large party at which guests shower attention and material possessions on the newlyweds. People who abuse their families and friends with scams like this deserve to be dropped off the social radar. And usually, when friends DO find out about the sham wedding—and they always find out—they do exactly that. Then the couple wonders why their social calendar is wide open.

At our reception, a relative of mine broke out in tears and caused quite a scene for some unknown reason. She did it again at the family breakfast the next morning. Six months later, we discovered the reason for her emotional display at our reception was because we had played a game at our reception which was similar to one that she had planned for her reception.

Many brides complain that they "had" to get married or now regret having a justice of the peace or registry wedding without all the fanfare of the reception. Life is full of regret, but unlike sporting events, we do not get to go back and see an instant replay or digitally change the outcome. However, this is not to say that the marriage cannot be celebrated. What we recommend to regretful brides is that they have an anniversary party to celebrate. Some brides want to renew their vows so that this time they can have the frou-frou dress and attendants. Nope. This won't fly. This brings us back to the Faux Wedding, the Sham Wedding, the Wedding for Show. A vow renewal is also a very special occasion and is done on a momentous anniversary (twenty-fifth and beyond). The protocol for a vow renewal is nothing like a wedding ceremony, so using the term "vow renewal" to try to put on a Faux Wedding won't do. Most couples who marry without all the frills choose their first or fifth anniversary to have a big celebration. And an anniversary is always a good thing to celebrate with friends and family.

BRIDEZILLA ANTITOXIN

Those helpful quick tips that keep the Bridezilla germs far away.

1. Never presume your guests will give you wedding presents. Yes, we know this seems to go against the concept of a registry, but as you register for gifts, don't presume that your guests will buy off the registry or even buy you gifts. The choice is theirs, not yours.

2. Cultivate gratefulness, because no one owes you anything on your wedding day. A gracious bride is truly a lovely woman not only on her wedding day but on all days.

3. It's not *your* day; it's *our* day to be shared with beloved family and friends whose presence brings you such happiness that you want to entertain them appropriately. *"Our"* means everyone who's involved with the wedding from the bride and groom to attendants to guests.

4. Guests are your treasured friends and family members. Money, a nice honeymoon, a new house, a big party—those are not reasons for inviting guests to a wedding. You've invited them because they are special people in your life and you want them to celebrate this occasion *with* you.

5. There are 365 days on the calendar and six billion people in the world. That's a good piece of trivia to remember when someone else says they're getting married on or near your chosen wedding date. We are all subject to a limited number of days for our special occasions.

6. Originality is wonderful, but if you buy a wedding gown off the rack or have it made from a pattern, chances are that someone else—maybe someone you know—will have the same gown. The difference will be in how you present yourself. There is no lovelier bride than the bride who is gracious and giving and who thinks of others before herself. Such a bride is often placed high on a pedestal and deservedly so.

7. Resources are finite. The resources we're talking about here are dollars. The groom has only so much, your guests have only so much, your families have only so much. It is not the goal of a gracious bride to spend every last dollar—and then some—of other people's money. The smart bride will fix a budget and then strive to come in *under* budget, and she will neither expect nor ask that others fund her wedding (see #4).

3) IT'S THE LITTLE THINGS THAT MEAN A LOT

CHAPTER THREE

Courtney was beside herself with anxiety. Her wedding planning had so far proceeded without incident, but now she was in a quandary. One bridesmaid refused to wear her hair in the bouffant hairstyle Courtney had chosen for all the attendants, Courtney had not been able to find napkins or a punch recipe in the shade of puce green she had chosen for her color, and worse, the florist was not able to get those green-tinged miniature roses imported from Tasmania after all.

The bridesmaid's rebellion was a dilemma because if Courtney laid on too thick a guilt trip, she risked having the bridesmaid quit altogether, and that would seriously ruin the look of the wedding she had envisioned by unbalancing the number of attendants. "A pox on her," Courtney cursed her bridesmaid under her breath, further cementing the Bridezilla's false and narcissistic notion that the wedding day is "All about me and what I want." Flowers, favors, napkins, the punch color—all must be perfect or the day is ruined. Thoughts of dear friends, cherished family, and a lifelong commitment are far, far away from the Bridezilla.

Details of her dress, the reception food, the fillings of the cake, and everything else wedding-related were the topics of discussion whenever she opened her mouth to anyone who was unfortunate enough to be standing nearby. She was so consumed in her plans and herself that she took the cake top to a family Christmas party so her relatives could see it before her wedding in March.

It's really rather presumptuous to think everyone is as interested in the wedding as the bride is. Such obsessing over the wedding planning details makes one wonder what this Bridezilla will talk about when her wedding is over. And then poor Bridezilla wonders why no one cares about her at all as the wedding day draws nearer. Perhaps because everyone has been heretofore so well informed about the details that there is simply no interest in her wedding anymore! Remember, mystery accomplishes much; discussing one's wedding ad nauseam is just boring.

At the reception, the bride, groom, and wedding party were in an area roped off from the guests. This was to indicate who could drink for free (the couple), and who had to pay (the guests).

Claire was a true Bridezilla. She argued with everyone about the details of her wedding and wouldn't listen to suggestions even after asking for input! She had to have THE BEST of everything, but nothing anyone else suggested was good enough. Even though she had almost a full year to plan her wedding, she put the blame on me if something didn't get done. As maid of honor, I wasn't doing my job, she would say. Going to law school and working full-time was just an excuse for me to get out of getting the dresses, ordering the flowers, finding the favors, and making hair appointments, according to her. When I planned my own wedding, I never read anywhere that those responsibilities belonged to the maid of honor.

Despite the months she had to get it all figured out, we attendants found out at the rehearsal dinner that she never ordered the dyeable shoes she said we HAD to wear because she didn't want to pay for them herself. So she threw a tantrum of childish proportions and demanded that we get those shoes and get them to match the electric teal-colored dresses we were to wear. We spent most of the wedding morning trying to find teal shoes. Finally, we gave up, bought matching white fabric shoes, went to a crafts store for spray paint, and painted those shoes electric teal.

While it is amazing that a bride will succumb to obsessing over shoe colors, what is more astonishing is that family and friends support her addiction to wedding planning minutia in the name of self-preservation. They will willingly, but perhaps grudgingly, rampage all over town trying to find that perfect shoe or a garter in an odd color or a particular brand of champagne lest the bride dissolve into a hormonal puddle of incoherent rants and raves. No one wants to be publicly identified as the sole source of a bride's wedding ruination, so when Bridezilla roars, the troops snap to attention, grovel in submission, and obey the call to serve. What would have worked well in this situation would have been to tell the bride that she was so lovely that no one would notice the bridesmaids' shoes. And as long as the bridesmaids weren't wearing army boots, then truly, no one would have noticed.

At the bride's request, we agreed to help her decorate the church basement where the reception would be held. It was stark and needed a lot of decorating to look festive. We had everything you can think of to decorate: white twinkle lights, yards and yards of white tulle, silk flowers, miles of streamers, and balloons and a helium tank. The air-conditioning in the basement wasn't due to be turned on until two hours before the wedding, so it was pretty warm and stuffy down there while we were busily working. After we had been at it for about an hour, we began to wonder where Gemma, the bride, was. We needed to ask her where she wanted some things placed. Another hour went by and still no Gemma. We spent over three hours decorating that basement, and she never showed up. We found out that while we were decorating and other friends were running HER last minute errands, she holed up in a comfy hotel room to watch TV. She said it was so that her hair and makeup would be perfect for "her day."

If a volunteer labor force is working more than three or four hours decorating and preparing for the wedding, it is considerate to serve them refreshments at your expense. There is nothing worse than spending six hours decorating the day before the wedding and still be expected to rustle up something to eat for lunch. Volunteers who give numerous hours of their time the day of the wedding should be thanked with a gift certificate to a restaurant, at the very least, along with the appropriate amount of verbal gratitude and gushing.

Sondra decided that she wanted the groom's mother and father to walk down the aisle together during the ceremony procession. Never mind that they had been divorced almost twenty-five years and had hardly spoken to each other since. Both had remarried some twenty-two years before and were very devoted to their current spouses. The groom's mother said she had made the mistake of walking down the aisle with the father of the groom once and she was not about to do it again. Sondra was very upset by this—she wanted her fiancé's parents to be together on her special day. In fact, she didn't even want the groom's step-father to wear a tux and be a part of the wedding party, even though he had been a part of groom's life since he was a kid.

The vision Sondra had of her fairy-tale wedding didn't include divorced parents and combined stepfamilies. So intent was she on suspending reality for a day that it didn't matter who she offended. Family members aren't toys to be rearranged and manipulated to suit one person's vision of her special day. The responsibility for reining in Sondra's runaway fantasy lay with her groom, who apparently had abdicated his role since the offense had spread throughout the family. This should have never gotten past the discussion stage between bride and groom.

Some couples like to have a special touch at the wedding reception by releasing white doves as symbols of their love. I am sure it is lovely to see the doves fly away together, but not at the wedding I attended.

The bride and groom had purchased two parakeets from the pet store in the bridal colors of green and yellow. The bride and groom stood on the lovely second-floor balcony of the bed and breakfast inn with all the guests watching from below. As the door of the birdcage was opened, the birds refused to come out. The bride and groom shook the cage and managed to extract the reluctant parakeets. The birds tumbled straight to the ground with a THUD! The pet store had clipped the parakeets' wings so they couldn't fly at all. It was horrifying. I hope the bride and groom didn't believe in bad omens!

We're not sure what's more pathetic: the fact that the poor birds couldn't fly or that the bride and groom were so wrapped up in their vision of the perfect wedding that they engaged in animal abuse by terrifying those poor birds with the intent of turning domestic critters into instant prey. With a little research, the couple would have learned that the only suitable birds for this type of stunt are rented homing pigeons, which are trained to return to their covey upon completion of their performance.

We know of another Bridezilla who intended to fly her pet pit bulls to the foreign country where her wedding was to take place so they could be the "flower children." In spite of concerns expressed about the long travel for the animals, the possibility of quarantine, and the unpredictability of pets in strange situations, she was adamant that her dream be fulfilled no matter what the costs.

We have no hesitation about dropping brides into Etiquette Hell for forcing animals or small children into acts to which they are not accustomed, for which they are not prepared, or that they do not want to do in the name of the Perfect Wedding.

> *Bethany gave her sisters specific details, including sketches, about how the getaway car should look. She also gave them all the decorations so they could do the job right. But when Bethany found out that her older brother's friends and some of the groomsmen had already decorated the car, she chewed him and the groomsmen out for "ruining her day."*

This is taking wedding planning obsession to new and dangerous heights when a Bridezilla actually draws out her dream rendition of the decorated getaway car and expects her subjects to decorate it according to her plans. It's legitimate to be concerned that the car decorators will create a tasteless, vulgar, trashy mess and truthfully, we all know that sometimes groomsmen are knuckle dragging, drool-dripping toads who are not above tasteless car "decorating." The answer to that is not to do what Bethany did but instead to conceal the getaway car until the very last moment so that juveniles—either in age or in actions—can't trash the honeymoon chariot.

Tasteful getaway car decorating can be a gently humorous send-off one's friends have elected to bestow, but one cannot insist that one is owed this and is therefore permitted to coordinate the decorating scheme. And if there are concerns that "tasteful" will not be the order of the day, then don't let anyone know which car is the getaway car.

When it was time to toss the bouquet and garter, the coordinator asked the bride for the bouquet. Toni had a smaller bouquet made specially for the tossing, but didn't know where it was. After much searching, the bridesmaids reported back that they couldn't find it either. The bride threw a major fit in front of the reception guests and screeched like a banshee witch that her bridesmaids were complete idiots and bridesmaids from hell.

The correct response to this Bridezilla would have been a dropped jaw with the question: "Surely you can't mean that?" If the Bridezilla continued with such rants, then the bridesmaids would certainly have every right to make a rapid yet dignified exit from the reception. This isn't a mature friend whose friendship is worth walking through hell for; this is a child in a wedding dress who probably had no business getting married since the occasion caused her to throw a tantrum over something that will, most likely, be fought over by prepubescent females and tossed in the trash within hours or days.

Her cousin, the bride, was on a budget, so Anna was surprised when she was informed that the bridesmaids' *dresses were going to cost $400. She thought that was rather steep but then thought it would be okay and paid for her dress. The bride then informed Anna that the shoes she was expected to buy would cost $125, the lipstick would be $45, and the matching nail polish would be another $40. Anna was getting concerned about all these expenditures that popped up since she too was planning her own wedding. She talked to the bride about her budget concerns, but the bride just brushed her off saying, "It's MY wedding. We'll do it as I say." A week later, the bride sent notes to the bridesmaids about her shower, reminding them of their obligation to give her a really good shower, and saying that they each needed to fork over at least $500 towards it or she wouldn't attend.*

An impending wedding is not an excuse to give the bride carte blanche to use her bridesmaids as play dolls and dress them as she pleases and at their expense. It's a bit obsessive to micromanage the colors and brands of lipstick and nail polish the bridesmaids will wear. The tragedy is that many bridesmaids do not know how to confront such behavior lest they create a conflict and destroy a friendship. They more or less go along with having every part of their personal toiletry, makeup, clothing, and hairstyle dictated by the bride who, in any other context, would probably never dream of treating her dearest friends and family as living dolls or children to be dressed in her own tastes. Their fear has its roots in reality, since they risk either a cursory dismissal or a major tantrum from the bride, because anyone who has invested considerable time in finding the "perfect" bridesmaids' dresses, shoes, nail polish, lipstick, and hairstyles is not going to give up her efforts easily. In addition, such minute attention to detail emphasizes the perception that the wedding is a theatrical production whose players must be clothed and made up according to the part they are playing. If the bridesmaids to this bride capitulated to her demands, the "honor" of standing up for this bride came with a price tag of over $1,000!

But let's get something straight right here and now: while Bridezilla may throw a tantrum over a bridesmaid who refuses to go along with emotional blackmail, extortion, and bodily changes all for the sake of a one-day event, those being ordered are in control of what they will and will not agree to do. Wails of "you'll ruin my wedding if..." should be ignored in most instances. Non-matching shoes, an undecorated getaway car, or a shower hosted within one's means will not—we repeat, *will not*—ruin anyone's wedding. Do not believe for one minute that it will.

I was a good friend of the groom so my wife and I were thrilled when he told us he was finally getting married. We told him that we had planned to take a few days off so we could be in town early. When his bride found out, she asked us to help decorate for the rehearsal dinner and the reception. When we arrived at the reception site by the lake, there was a list of things to do including yard work and paint touch-ups. The groomsmen and some of their wives were also there so everyone pitched in to do the yard work, set up tiki torches, sweep sidewalks and so on. When my *wife said she wasn't able to do heavy work, the bride said, "Fine, you can help me with the flowers." My wife was more than willing to help with the flowers until the bride told her that she would need to go back into a neighborhood area and <u>steal</u> flowers from people's gardens and lawns!!! And since my wife wasn't able to pitch in with the "heavy" work the bride then asked her to take charge of the rehearsal dinner barbeque. This meant cooking, serving and cleanup afterward. We did it more out of shock than anything else, but my friendship with the groom went downhill after that.*

In stealing flowers from neighboring gardens, the Bridezilla failed in one major area: she obviously didn't care about the condition, color, or type of flowers. However, this Bridezilla scores big points in the "all about me" category, since she is willing to put everybody else's reputation on the line by having them steal the flowers.

The day before the wedding is not the time to be telling your volunteer helpers that lawn care and meal preparation are an expected part of their gift of labor. This bride had to have known what was required, but she waited until the last possible moment to spring this on her friends, knowing that it is human nature not to want to be the cause of a "scene" or be the lynchpin that may ruin a friend's wedding day.

The proper course of action here would have been for all the attendants to attempt to have a conversation with the bride and groom and come to an agreement about what realistically could be accomplished, what wasn't necessary (i.e. flowers for the rehearsal dinner), and what was unacceptable (stealing). Sometimes taking what appears to be the easy way out (refusing to do another person's dirty work) is actually taking the moral road.

For her bachelorette party, Coral insisted on having "props" to wear out to the clubs, meaning she wanted all of us to wear t-shirts that read, "Suck for a buck," with hard candies sewn onto them. The idea was that random guys at the club/bar would give us a dollar in exchange for them biting the candy off the front of the t-shirt, no matter where the candy was positioned on the shirt. No thanks. She wanted us to wear nametags that were in the shape of penises. She wanted us to wear bras on the outside of our clothes and little penis earrings. She also wanted all of us to make out with male strippers. When I told her that I thought that was nasty and that I was engaged, she said, "So what? You're not married yet. So you're single. Besides, it's MY night!"

There are several celebratory functions associated with a wedding for which the bride and groom are not responsible. Those events are engagement parties, showers, rehearsal dinners, and bachelor/bachelorette parties. Hosting responsibilities fall to parents, siblings, friends, or extended family as appropriate for each particular event. The bride and groom are expected to behave like the

The bride, my twin sister, told each bridesmaid that the dress would cost $140 and to pay her directly. However, she told me the dress would cost $190. After I found out what the dress really cost, I asked her why she had told me it would cost so much more. She replied that she needed some extra funds for her shoes and she didn't want to dun her best friends.

proper guests of honor at these functions and not to dictate how the party should be executed. If asked for suggestions, their input can be considered, but ultimately the decisions for how the party will be hosted rests with the host or hostess.

People almost expect brides to obsess over the attire of the bridesmaids in the wedding, but it is extreme to dictate what they wear and do at a bachelorette party. This bride has fallen for the misconception that everything associated with her wedding day is "mine" to the point at which it is not just "my day" but "my night" as well. Victims of this type of Bridezilla must gird themselves against an onslaught of guilt and manipulative whines more typical of a bratty three-year-old than an adult woman. It is OK to tell a Bridezilla, "No, I don't think that is appropriate," and then ignore the tantrums. And if the tantrums persist, it's perfectly fine to suggest alternatives, but this is done more successfully if *all* the bridesmaids are in full agreement to the alternatives, leaving the Bridezilla no choice but to go along with something more reasonable or to go alone.

But in the final analysis, a bachelorette party is not a requirement for a successful wedding. Neither are showers, teas, engagement parties, or other celebratory events. The successful wedding is one in which the guests are treated well, the bride and groom behave themselves, and everyone leaves the event wishing they didn't have to go.

At the reception, there were some so-so floral arrangements on each table. Next to each arrangement was a card. Thinking that the florist neglected to clean up, I picked up a card, which turned out to be a small envelope. The envelope had "Centerpiece" written on the outside. Inside was a small card that read, "If you would like to take this arrangement home, please write a check for $30 to the happy couple so you can have a memento of their special day."

This couple didn't miss any opportunity to cash in on the wedding and make a few extra bucks. Do people really sit up at night devising creative ways to extract more cash from their guests? Yes, they do. From the enclosure of registry cards in invitations to outright demands of cash ("because we don't want five toasters"), we have an extra-special warm place in Etiquette Hell for those couples who choose to use such a precious time as a means for extortion. Weddings are not fundraising events at which decorations may be sold to the highest bidder. We suggest that one leave the floral arrangement but take the card as a memento of a tacky reception.

BRIDEZILLA ANTITOXIN

Those helpful quick tips that keep the Bridezilla
germs far away.

1. As the saying goes, don't sweat the small stuff. The result at
the end of the day is that you are married, with or without all
the wedding planning minutia.

2. If you have spent far more time in planning wedding details
than on premarital counseling, you should probably re-exam-
ine your priorities. The emphasis should be on planning a
successful *marriage*, not a successful one-day extravaganza.

3. Your bridesmaids are not your personal dress-up dollies to
attire according to your whims. It is neither tacky nor ugly to
let bridesmaids choose the hairstyles, jewelry, and makeup
that they believe accentuate their best features.

4. Your bridesmaids and groomsmen are not your personal
servants to order as you wish. Ask, with plenty of notice, if you
need something tended to. Be prepared to hear "no" and have
a backup plan ready, even if it means (gasp!) paying for that
help. And if your bridesmaids and groomsmen do agree to
help with whatever task you've asked of them, then please
show the appropriate amount of gratitude.

5. What you plan today will become the family joke two decades
from now. Styles change and tastes evolve, and after a decade
of married life that wedding photo album will become the
archive of your obsessiveness. "Butt bows! You actually made
your bridesmaids wear dresses with butt bows the size of
angel wings? HAHAHAHAHA!" Simplicity is timeless, but if
you choose over-the-top styles, just remember—you were
warned!

6. A wedding ceremony is a special event in recognition of two people who make a mature, conscious decision to forge through life together. It is a happy day, a day to celebrate. Your wedding ceremony is not a theatrical production needing dictatorial direction lest a bad "opening day" portend a bad start to the marriage.

7. Your wedding is important to you. It is also important to family and friends, but it is not nearly as interesting in detail as it is to you. The way to keep good friends is to remain as "normal" as possible during the wedding planning. Using wedding planning as an excuse—as ANY excuse—will not endear you to those around you. Your friends will be far more excited about your wedding if you keep the details to yourself, letting them see the fruits of your hard work on the wedding day.

BRIDEZILLA ANTIBIOTIC
For Bridesmaids, Family, and Friends

1. Bridesmaids, you do not have to cater to every whim of the bride. Use reasonable and sound judgment when it comes to money and off-the-wall requests. In the presence of a true Bridezilla, someone needs to be the voice of reason.

2. Family members, likewise for you. While it's one thing to bend over backward for someone who truly appreciates your efforts, being a good mother/father/sister/brother/cousin/ whoever does not require you to be a doormat to an ungrateful bride.

3. Friends, you are not required to bow to the bride and groom as if they were Queen and King. You've been invited to share in the celebration. You are guests. You are to be treated kindly.

At the first sign of extortion, "my way or the highway" behaviors, or other out-of-the-ordinary actions, just step back and away. Being a good friend would have you keep your wits about you while others are going off the deep end. (With apologies to Rudyard Kipling for the loose paraphrase.)

4) SHOWER ME WITH GIFTS, OR I WILL DESTROY TOKYO

CHAPTER FOUR

The assault on her guests' wallets was taking on all the signs of a military campaign. With her glasses slipping far down her nose in deep concentration, Courtney was comparing her guest list with her registries and comparing the financial health of each intended guest, as she perceived it, with her wedding budget balance sheet. Courtney was on a mission. A mission to make a profit from her wedding by extracting more cash and booty from her guests than it cost her to execute the wedding. So far, her diabolical plans had been progressing quite nicely. Confused guests had actually shown up *with gifts* at the engagement party that she had arranged for herself! Courtney congratulated herself on having successfully manipulated her bridesmaids, her friends, her mother, her sister, and her mother's friends into hosting not one bridal shower but five! Crying, pouting, throwing tantrums, and generally looking dejected were just a few of the weapons in the arsenal of this most fiendish of Bridezillas.

I was a clerk in a bridal registry department for two years. I remember this one bride who really thought it was just fine to put a note on her registry saying, "The china costs $90 for each place setting. If you are unable to give us at least one full place setting, then please don't give us anything." We left the note off.

Oh, the presumptuousness of it! As if the bride can direct people what to get! Bridal registries have become a necessary evil originally created as a marketing tool by department stores and now slyly justified as an aid to befuddled guests who cannot seem to think of a single gift to give the bridal couple. Etiquette-challenged retailers have been known to hand brides registry cards and encourage their inclusion in the wedding invitation, which is a grave faux pas landing the bride into that extra warm spot in Etiquette Hell. Proper etiquette is not to presume one will receive wedding gifts in the first place, so as to avoid the progression to believing that one may dictate guests' gift giving. The bride in this story believes the gifts she gets are rightfully owed to her and that she can set the parameters of her guests' giving. Kudos to this department store staff for refusing her greedy and presumptuous request!

> My best friend and his girlfriend were married last year. Being notoriously frugal-minded in spite of their extravagant incomes, we were all surprised to see very expensive items on their gift registry. When gifts were being opened at the morning-after brunch, the bride and groom wouldn't let anyone touch or hold the more expensive gifts. When someone tried to open a box of expensive crystal goblets, we learned the reason for their hands-off policy. They had registered for a lot of expensive things because they wanted to return them all and get store credit toward new furniture.

This type of underhanded manipulation of the gift giving process is gaining popularity as more people marry later in life thus combining two complete households that are lacking in nothing. Cash

At the shower, the bride received two very lovely (and expensive) monogrammed towels. The bride threw up her arms and said that she hoped someone had enough brains to give her at least two more towels to make a full set.

then becomes a more advantageous gift, but to ask directly for cash gifts is rude, so the above dirty tactic is often used as a poor substitute. It's a major etiquette faux pas, because it is a direct slap in the face of the guests, many of whom spent time, energy, and thought seeking out the registry, choosing a gift (either off the registry or selecting something special), and having it wrapped and sent, only to discover the effort was for naught. It is simply the bridal version of money laundering by using the store registry to convert gifts to cash. Make a mental note when you encounter such a couple and resolve not to buy them any housewarming or baby shower gifts since you will have had firsthand experience in their schemes. Also note that many stores are on to couples who attempt this money-laundering scheme and will not permit returns for cash, only for store credit at the lowest price that the item has been sold for since arriving in inventory. That means if a crystal vase ever went on sale for half price, the store credit would be much less than one is anticipating. Many stores will not permit returns of items unless the couple was actually registered there, and again, the only thing to be gained is store credit, not cash.

At her shower, she received several generous and beautiful gifts from the guests, i.e., sterling silver bowls, gourmet *cookware, entire barware sets, Baccarat crystal, Wedgwood china, etc. However, instead of being gracious, she dismissed everyone with a hesitant "thanks" and then spent the rest of the day going over and over who gave what and how much each gift was worth! Saying things like, "Jane Doe bought me a food processor. That's probably around $200," was common, but she never expressed any appreciation for the _people_ who gave the gifts or for the hostesses of the shower. Having been one of her hostesses and having given her a nice gift, I was none too pleased by her vulgar attitude.*

As the contributor of this story conveys so well, people do take offense at ungratefulness in response to their generosity. No one likes to feel like her sole worth to the bride or groom is predicated upon the value of the gift she gave. Brides like this will wonder in later years why they have so few friends or why the friends they have are such shallow people. In the end, we all get the friends we deserve, and viewing people on the basis of the value of the wedding gift is a surefire way to lose friends. The bride also appeared not to know that shower gifts are supposed to be token gifts, not large and lavish ones. That so many people gave beyond the "token" status should have made her even more grateful to have been thought of so highly-once upon a time, that is.

It seems like all the showers I've attended lately have one strange thing in common. As the guests would arrive, the hostesses would hand them envelopes and instruct them to put their names and addresses on the envelopes so that the bride could send them a thank-you note. Don't you think that if the guests could take the time to go shopping, select a gift, wrap it and bring it to the shower, the bride could personally address the envelopes? This is really tacky!

This isn't just tacky; it's also lazy and selfish. It's a statement by the bride that her time is much more valuable than her guests' and that she can't be bothered with lowering herself to the task of handwriting and properly addressing a personal note of thanks. If the bride didn't dream up the idea, it's often the brainstorm of the shower organizer who herself hated the notion of being burdened with expressing thanks. In that case, the bride should have gently put her foot down by saying to her hostess, "Oh, but it's important that I write the notes myself, all the way down to the envelopes."

Gift giving often requires an investment in time by the giver to travel to a store, spend time choosing an appropriate gift, wrap it, and then transport it to the shower or send it to the bride's home prior to the wedding. Then to be required to address one's own thank-you note envelope is just insulting. Other tacky ploys, such as writing generic "one-size-fits-all" notes, using preprinted "Thank you for the gift" notes, or (gasp!) using a Web service to write and send thank-you notes will also readily plop a Bridezilla into Etiquette Hell, where she will be forced to write thank-you notes for the most horrific gifts imaginable for all eternity.

The bride registered for expensive gifts at all the most expensive stores. At her shower, when she received a gift that was not listed on her registry, she openly pouted about it. One guest had gone to one of the expensive stores to check out her registry and then went to a less-expensive department store to get a pair of her crystal wine glasses. Maybe she made a mistake or maybe the department store did. But it was embarrassing for all the guests when the bride held up one of the wine glasses to the light in the window and proclaimed, "This is NOT my pattern!"

Again, the inherent problem of registries is that they are based on the belief that the guests will be giving gifts and that the gift giving can be directed by the intended recipient. The temptation exists to slide further down the slippery slope into ungrateful Bridezillaism when guests eschew the registry in favor of finding something they think would be more appropriate to give. And heaven forbid if a guest attempts to purchase a gift from the registry at another store that happens to be more convenient, either in distance or cost!

Although the purpose of a shower is to shower the bride with gifts, the bride still

After flying across the country, spending outrageous amounts of money on a bridesmaid's outfit, and running errands for the couple, the groom pulled me aside after the wedding and demanded to know where I bought the gift I gave them so he could return it for cash.

has the social responsibility to be wonderfully surprised and appropriately grateful for each gift she receives.

I recently attended a shower where, despite receiving gifts from her own registry, the bride was petulant and complained about each gift given to her. She would open the present, look at the gift giver and dolefully comment, "I don't like this. You'll have to return and exchange it."

The guest's proper response to such a wretched, ungrateful declaration would be to say, "Of course. I'll take care of it," and promptly take possession of the gift, which she would return for a cash refund to keep all to herself. Such a bride does not deserve any gift. Brides must remember that the only thing they need to say upon receiving an unwanted object is, "How thoughtful! How original! Thank you!" Anything other than a sincere attempt to be grateful just won't do.

A few weeks after the wedding, I had lunch with the bride and was startled when she started to comment about which guests gave her presents and how much each present cost. She whined about several people who sent gifts that she guessed were worth less than $25. She said that she had been expecting a present worth at least $50 or more, since the reception dinner cost $42 per person, and there had been all those other expenses like the centerpieces, favors, the band and so on. I stared in disbelief as she continued on and said some couples should have given her more expensive presents because as a "couple" they cost *double for the dinner, so the value of their presents should have been double. I spent close to $130 on set of trendy cooking utensils and said I hope she got one or two of the pots and pans from the matching cookware set, and she said, "Oh yes, we did! We got everything in the set! It was worth $600, and we only paid $42 to let her come to the wedding!!"*

In the years Etiquette Hell has been in existence, we never cease to be amazed at how many people believe the cost of the wedding gift should equal or surpass the cost of the reception meal, as if the guests are supposed to experience some transcendental realization upon opening the invitation that each guest's attendance equals a certain sum of expense by the hosts. Once the bride begins presuming guests owe a wedding gift, it is often a natural progression to believe that one's wedding is a business venture in which the profits must exceed the initial capital investment, which quite often has been made by family and not the bride and groom themselves. It makes it easy for couples to overextend the wedding budget if they expect to get an equal or greater return on their money in the form of cash gifts and material possessions. The obvious result is that guests are looked upon as commodities or profit-generating entities rather than as beloved friends and family.

About four months before the wedding I found my answering machine tape crammed with several messages. A few were for me but most were from the bride leaving messages for my roommate Elizabeth, who was her maid of honor. Screaming. Wailing. Hollering. It seems she was under the *impression that Elizabeth had not arranged a bridal shower for her. She spent several minutes of answering machine tape <u>screaming</u> into the machine about Elizabeth's "failure" to live up to the duties of a maid of honor. Then she hung up.*

Then she called again and screamed some more. I assumed she got the wrong answering machine. Nope. In her last message, she admitted that she couldn't get through to Elizabeth so she deliberately left the messages on my machine hoping that dragging in a third party would convey how upset she was! Did I mention that Elizabeth had actually knocked herself out organizing a beautiful bridal shower, but that it was to be a surprise party?

Elizabeth probably wondered if she was planning a bridal shower for an adult or a terrible-twos toddler. Screaming, wailing, and throwing tantrums are not unexpected in undisciplined toddlers, but we presume people have outgrown such self-absorbed, immature, and manipulative behavior by the time they reach marrying age. This bride's lack of discretion in her presumptions and subsequent treatment of a friend are usually the things that make for one lonely person when all is said and done. Claiming wedding planning "stress" as the exacerbating source for tantrums is not an acceptable excuse. Life is full of stressful occasions now and in the future—moving, births, illness, job changes, family crises, and so on may not be used as excuses to rant at others. This bride, upon realizing her grievous error, should have apologized most profusely to Elizabeth and to Elizabeth's friend and made it her personal mission to repent for her ill behavior until the end of time, not through continued apology, but with gracious behavior and kind friendship. Failing an apology, Elizabeth should note this bride's behavior and stay clear of her for all future "spotlight" events, like birthday parties, housewarmings, and baby showers for hypothetical future children.

She said, "I'm getting a bachelorette party, right?" I replied out of obligation, "Yes." She asked, "I'm getting a limo, right?" I said, "No, we can't afford a limo." She replied that she didn't understand. She also told me where the bachelorette party should be, how she thought all the girls should ride in a limo, and how she expected one of those fake "bride-to-be" veils that young, 21-year-old college girls wear for their bachelorette parties. (Keep in mind, Bridezilla was 35 at the time.) I bit my tongue and said nothing. I was shocked that she was dictating to me how her so-called surprise bachelorette party was going to be— as if she should have anything to say about it at all—or that she assumed she was getting one at all.

The bachelorette party is a degradation of society that ought to be stopped right this minute. It grew out of petty retaliation against grooms and their pals who spent the night before their wedding getting smashed and getting teased (and then some) by scantily clad (if even clad!) dancers in a strip joint. After all, what's good for the goose.... It's astonishing that supposedly mature individuals who have decided they can't live without another can actually go out the night before they take solemn vows and live as if there is no moral standard and no consequence to their actions. Remember, one day that groom will be somebody's daddy, and that bride will be somebody's mommy. What a horrible legacy to have for one's children. In this particular episode, however, the situation is compounded by the sheer immaturity of the bride. Our Bridezilla is digressing into the "look-at-me-I'm-a-princess" mindset by wanting her carriage and play costume and dictating how her royal treatment will be handled. She doesn't belong in a wedding; she belongs back in her playpen where she can make believe she's a princess to her little pink heart's content.

I attended a bridal shower for which my grandmother was one of four hostesses. Being held on a Saturday afternoon, the hostesses decided that punch, tea, and a pretty cake were enough for refreshments. Bridezilla found out about the menu from one of the other hostesses and called my grandmother to tell her what foods she should be serving instead: meatballs, vegetable crudités, finger sandwiches, cheese and crackers, crab cakes, imported wine, and more. My grandmother was taken aback but stated that for an afternoon party, a "meal" wasn't called for, just light refreshments. Bridezilla decided this just would not do so she took matters into her own hands. She told friends who would be attending the shower to bring the food items she wanted. She never conferred with the shower hostesses about this change in plans so when she arrived at the shower with her food-bearing friends in tow, she relegated the cake and punch to the kitchen counter. When the all the guests arrived, none were in the mood for the heavier foods so the cake and punch made their way out of obscurity and were a huge hit, much to the dismay of Bridezilla.

A wedding is an exciting time period in a person's life and an opportunity for many celebratory functions. Despite the temptation to believe that since this is the bride's "special day" and everything must be subordinate to her desires, wishes, and plans, there are some wedding-related functions that are outside the jurisdiction of the bride, groom, or their families to plan and execute. The bride is a guest of honor at any shower hosted for her, and the proper behavior of a guest of honor is to enjoy the party without worrying one pretty little hair on her bridal head about any of the details. Only a Bridezilla would begin to presume that she can have a significant role in determining the menu, location, or games played.

In this true tale of bridal bamboozlement, the hostesses probably should have been more responsive, since the bride was clearly in need of a stronger statement to quash the notion that Bridezilla rules. The smart hostess would have turned into a world-class diplomat and said, "Oh, but dear, I've already made such wonderful plans and wait until you see this cake! You're sweet to offer to do more, but I simply won't hear of it. This is my treat to you, so

The sign posted at the exit door at a reception read:

The party is over

No need to pout

Just leave your gift

And get the hell out!

you just relax and leave everything to me!" Also, her friends should have checked with the hostesses about food needs. Upon calling the hostesses, the friends would have learned that they need not trouble themselves with any of the details as they were already being handled.

Fearing that some obtuse wedding dreams might be shattered should not deter the hostesses or friends from doing the right thing. Some "dreams" are actually nightmares in reality and in need of some readjustments. Unfortunately, the capitulation to the Bridezilla went so far that these poor ladies were no longer hostesses and friends but merely caterers preparing food for a shower planned entirely by the bride.

Since a friend in my large social group was getting married fairly close to my wedding date, our mutual friends decided to give us a joint shower. I thought it was a great idea. By the time our shower was held, we were about six weeks away from Nancy's wedding and ten weeks before mine. The shower was very nice and very generous of our friends since they all showed up with gifts for both of us.

When most of the guests had left, I stayed behind to help my friends, the hostesses, with some clean up. I also wanted to give each of them a little gift of appreciation. While we were talking, we realized that none of us had been invited to Nancy's wedding! Only one person who attended the shower actually received a wedding invitation. We had just thought that Nancy hadn't sent them out yet.

After talking with the one person who had been invited, we learned that Nancy had decided that she didn't feel close enough with any of us so we wouldn't be invited to the wedding. She had, however, felt close enough to us to let us throw her a bridal shower and bestow her with gifts! She could have just let us know that she was having a small, intimate wedding, and that although she appreciated the gesture, she really couldn't accept the offer of a shower. But noooo, she decided to take advantage of the situation and gift grub from people she didn't feel "close to." We were shocked. One of our mutual friends in the group learned about the situation and immediately returned the wedding gift she had purchased for Nancy after the shower. After all, she too had been expecting a wedding invitation that was never going to come.

Nancy is a classic Bridezilla who placed a greater priority on the gifts than the givers. In the years to come, Nancy will wonder why her circle of friends has shrunk even smaller as word of her despicable deed spreads throughout the social grapevine and she is avoided like a bad cold. While it may seem odd that one act such as this would brand her for life, this type of action is generally not limited to just weddings; the bride who would pull something like this and feel she has gotten away with it usually has a track record of such antics. Things would have been so different had she demurred the offer of a shower in her honor. Had the hostesses wanted to fete her anyway, a more appropriate event would have been a tea, which does not carry the obligation of gifts. This story illustrates why it's so important for the hostess to confer with the bride on the guest list to insure that everyone on the shower guest list is also invited to the wedding, lest the hostess also be thought guilty of some sort of Bridezilla collusion.

I received an invitation to a bridal shower for a co-worker. Listed on the invitation were the four places the bride was registered for wedding gifts. Additionally, we were requested to bring a bottle of champagne. "OK," I thought, "no problem." Then one of the hostesses called and asked me to bring a dish to pass. "OK," I thought, "no problem." I showed up for the shower with a gift, champagne, and a dish to pass.

The house looked beautiful. I noticed right away that the only people invited were people from work—about thirty-three of us—and the bride's mother. We played games and had refreshments. Then the raffle for the champagne: whoever brought a bottle (thirty bottles were brought) got her name put into a raffle for a gift basket containing one bottle of champagne and assorted treats. Come to find out, the rest of the champagne we had brought was for the wedding reception toast. "Great idea," I thought. Then the bride opened all the gifts, which took over two hours.

After that was over, the hostess got everyone's attention to make an announcement at the bride's request. She said, "The bride regrets not being able to invite everyone she wanted, so this is her way of sharing her joy with those who won't be attending the wedding and reception."

This is one of our personal favorites of all the Etiquette Hell stories! The ability to lure thirty of her co-workers to cheerfully and willingly attend a shower bearing food, gifts, and bottles of champagne is truly an awe-inspiring example of cunning, charm, and deceit by an accomplished Bridezilla. It was audacious enough to invite to a shower people that she had no intention of inviting to the wedding and reception, but to then ask them to cater the shower was incredibly presumptuous. The coup de grace was to lie to her shower guests that she wanted them to "share in her joy," as if being abused for food, champagne, and shower gifts is a far more pleasurable and joyous experience than attending the wedding and reception as real guests.

Once recovered from the shock of being used, one can hear one of the guests saying, "My champagne and I are simply too dear to be parted, and I'm sure my bottle would not want to go a wedding without me so I'll decline your kind invitation to the wedding for it." Then one can see this guest resolutely exiting the shower with champagne in hand. This presumes one has the presence of mind to actually come up with something audible while one's jaw is still on the floor. Undoubtedly the guests at this shower were too stunned to pick up their jaws to speak, leaving the shower in an incredulous silence. They had been in the horrific presence of a world-class Bridezilla. Truly, such is an unforgettable moment.

One of our department managers finally decided to marry his long-time girlfriend, so I thought it would be nice to arrange a shower for them at our office. I helped arrange a cake-and-punch party, organized a collection from the staff (our staff of twenty-five managed to come up with almost $600), purchased, wrapped, and hauled gifts to the office, and generally knocked myself out to plan and execute this event for our manager and his fiancée.

But the bride had a fit. I had purchased a set of cookware for them, but it wasn't the same brand as she had requested on her registry! The brand on the registry was a store brand; the store was closing it out, and there was no way to purchase it anymore. I purchased a different set instead.

Bridezilla angrily shouted across the room after opening the large box of cookware, "We didn't register for this! Now we'll have to take it back! Why did you buy it for us? Are you stupid?" Everything else purchased had been listed on her registry; she pouted her way through opening the rest of the gifts and refused to speak to any of the co-workers present. She didn't even give a verbal "thank you" for the shower, the gifts, or anything else.

Since the sight of this set of cookware was an offense to the bride's eyes, the proper reaction to her would have been to say, "Oh, dear. You are quite right. What was I thinking? I'll just take that cookware back. You don't need to worry about it anymore." Without further fuss or drama, the guest would take possession of the evil cookware. What would not be told to the bride is that the evil cookware would be returned for a cash refund to be redistributed back to the employees. The Etiquette Hell rule is that one does not feed the beasts lest their boorish behavior become entrenched or socially sanctioned.

At the reception, the bride was talking with a friend about another friend who had been unable to travel to the wedding. The bride said, "It doesn't matter that much because he sent a check for $200. That's all that counts."

On the day of the bridal shower, the bride took the mother of the groom aside and confided to her that in the event she decided to dump the groom before the wedding, she planned to keep all the gifts for herself.

Etiquette and decency require one to return all shower and wedding gifts if the wedding is called off or indefinitely postponed. Shower and wedding gifts are intended to celebrate new married life together, and if that event does not transpire, every effort must be made to return them. Of course, decency also requires that one does not confide a contrary intent to one's future mother-in-law.

As a corollary, we are often asked about the disposition of gifts if the marriage doesn't last. Once the "I do's" are exchanged, the gifts belong to the couple. If the marriage doesn't last more than a few weeks, the gifts are still theirs. Of course, if the marriage doesn't make it past the honeymoon (literally), one would hope that some good sense and politeness would prevail and the gifts would be sent back to the guests. It's not required by the very strictest of etiquette standards, but it's never incorrect to do that which is truly correct.

I was a little unnerved after calling my friend's shower hostess to find out where the happy couple had registered; she reeled off a list of about six stores. My friend was in her mid-30s, divorced, making a six-figure income, and possessed a fully-stocked apartment, which she shared with her intended. I was also a little surprised when the hostess cheerfully warbled on, saying, "The wedding is going to be a small affair, mostly family, you see, so this way all of the bride's friends who can't come to the wedding can still share part of the fun!"

Eh!? Oh, well, pettiness never got anyone anywhere, so I duly trudged off to purchase a shower gift from her registry list. When I got to the shower, there were about twenty-five other women there, and we set to chatting, brunching, and showering amid plastic platters of food from the local supermarket deli. The groom-to-be was the special invited guest for the finale of the shower, and in due time he arrived.

Then came the corker. They gathered us all together and announced amid much smiling and cuddling that they weren't going to get married after all—it was just too expensive for them to do it up the way they wanted to, so they were going to wait a year or two! The shower broke up with the guests making a frosty exit.

When you envision "sharing some fun," does the thought even cross your mind that attending a wedding shower for someone who is not getting married would fit those "fun" parameters? Of course not. "Share my joy/fun" is fast becoming a euphemism for, "I hope you get a vicarious thrill out of seeing me extract gifts from people I would never invite to my wedding. Like you." The horrible thing about this is that the couple honestly seemed to think that their friends would not mind being lied to, abused, and insulted. Bridezilla and Groomonster, enjoy your stay in Etiquette Hell.

The invitations were sent out for a bridal shower hosted by the mother of the bride. The invitation included a note which said to send $20 to the bride's mother, and she would make all the arrangements. The shower was held at a tearoom, and the $20 paid for the tea and scones and all the gifts, which had been purchased and wrapped by the mother of the bride. The bride wasn't the least bit surprised by any of this, but the guests were... they finally got to see what they had paid for!

There is a reason why etiquette frowns heavily on showers hosted by immediate family members, and this story illustrates it well. There is a temptation for moms, sisters, and sisters-in-law to have a misplaced vested interest in seeing a family member well-endowed with the proper parties and loads of gifts. It has the appearance of greed, even when none may exist, and gives the perception that one's friends and extended family will not rise to the occasion to host a shower, thus requiring the desperate act of recruiting family members.

There is a mistaken belief that the maid/matron of honor has the mandatory responsibility for hosting a bridal shower. While customary in a traditional sense, it is not an obligatory duty. If the bridesmaids are scattered to and fro, are in college, have heavy work schedules, or have families of their own, it's often logistically difficult and unfeasible to have a bridesmaids' shower, and no offense should be taken by the bride, especially since she is the one who choose bridesmaids who may not have oodles of time on their hands. Times have changed, and bridesmaids these days are usually not the childhood gal pals who still live in the neighborhood.

There are also other factors to consider. The very young bride, or the bride who has not had the thrill of being a bridesmaid herself, may select equally young and inexperienced bridesmaids who are not aware of their traditional duties. And there is that rare instance in which the bride has been so horrible to her bridesmaids that they are not inclined to do more than the absolute minimum, which is walk down the aisle and pose for pictures. The simple fact is that a bride is not "entitled" to a shower. Fortunately, most brides are not Bridezillas and are feted with perfectly lovely showers without resorting to breathing fire upon all creation to get one.

BRIDEZILLA ANTITOXIN

Those helpful quick tips that keep the Bridezilla germs far away.

1. One shower is great. Two showers are nice. Three showers are approaching greedy. Four showers make a Bridezilla.

2. The bride does not have to accept every offer for a shower and probably should not if she is blessedly popular. The hostess who is turned down for a shower may offer to host a non-gifting tea or cocktail party instead. If the bride refuses, then drop the matter. Surprise—there will be some brides who do not want a lot of pre-wedding hoopla. Bless their little hearts!

3. The bride and hostess need to review the shower guest list together to make sure that 1) everyone invited to the shower is also invited to the wedding, and 2) no one is invited to the shower who has already been invited to another shower for the same bride.

4. Office showers are exempt from some of the rules. If co-workers are completely aware that they are not invited to the wedding and want to give a shower anyway, they may, and the bride does not need to feel shamed into inviting them to the wedding.

5. Family does not host showers. Not moms, future mothers-in-law, stepmoms, sisters (see exception below), or daughters.

6. Exceptions to the family does not host showers rule:

    a) Sisters may co-host if they are also bridesmaids. But the shower should be held in a non-family location.

    b) The groom's mother may host a shower if the bride is from far, far away and is moving to the groom's hometown and knows no one at all. The guests should be those who are in the groom's social circle and would be contemporaries of the bride and groom. This would double as the bride's introduction into the community.

c) Family may host a shower if the guest list is comprised of family only. Blood relatives.

7. Brides do not plan any part of their shower. Their pre-party contribution is to agree to a date and to review the guest list, and nothing more.

8. The multi-married bride should forgo showers. Of course, if the bride left behind all her worldly possessions when leaving a bad first marriage, then it would be appropriate to shower her for her new beginning. The same holds true for a widow who suffered total household devastation. But those who are doing nicely on their own prior to marrying again should exercise restraint and maturity and forgo the showers, since the purpose of a shower is to help the unestablished couple set up a home. This does not prevent the bride's friends from feting her with a tea, luncheon or other event if they wish.

9. Guests do not pay for the privilege of attending a shower. They are not to be asked to bring food and drink or to pay for the food and drink if the shower is held at a restaurant. The hostesses are entirely responsible for hosting the shower, and that includes footing the bill. If there are budgetary concerns, one may host a simple and elegant shower with nothing more than cake and punch in one's home. A shower need not be expensive to be exquisite.

10. Registry information is never included in shower invitations. The invitation may specify a theme, such as "kitchen shower," "tool shed shower," "lingerie shower," and so on, but never the location of a registry. Guests are always free to shop where they will and purchase what they will. If a guest wants to know registry information, the guest will ask.

11. FYI: Gifts at a shower are not lavish. Gifts are typically small and more on the token side. After all, shower guests will also be wedding guests and are obligated to send a more significant wedding gift as well.

12. While a verbal expression of thanks for a gift received at a shower is sufficient, most people don't know that and get *really* offended if a note of thanks is not sent. Send thank-you notes. Promptly. Thank-you notes are written on plain paper or note cards. They do not ever come preprinted, not even with THANK YOU screaming across the front. Thank-you notes are always handwritten unless one has a disability and must use a typewriter. Thank-you notes are to be in the mail absolutely no later than two weeks after the shower and certainly before the wedding. If the shower was co-ed, the groom is expected write his share of the thanks. But if he doesn't, then the bride must pick up the slack and make sure that everyone is duly thanked.

13. Speaking of thanks, brides must thank their hostesses in writing. Those notes should be the first ones written and mailed. It is not necessary to give "hostess gifts," but one may do so if so inclined. Such a gift could be a bouquet of flowers, a box of candy, or some other gift the bride knows the hostess will enjoy.

5) MEDDLE NOT IN THE AFFAIRS OF BRIDEZILLA FOR YOU ARE CRUNCHY & GOOD WITH KETCHUP

CHAPTER FIVE

Courtney sat pondering her dilemma. There was murmured mutiny brewing within the ranks of her eight bridesmaids, and Courtney had to quell it quickly or abandon her vision of her perfect wedding.

"What's wrong with my friends anyway?" Courtney asked herself. "I mean, like, what's the big deal about the designer bridesmaids' dresses? I like them."

It had not occurred to Courtney that her friends and sisters might not appreciate wearing an unflattering strapless dress with butt bows the size of hang glider wings on their fannies of varying widths. To their thinking, they were going to look like a squadron of puce-colored kites processing down the cathedral aisle.

But it wasn't the dresses alone that stirred the pot of discontent among the bridesmaids. Like adding weights on a scale, the balance of goodwill the bridesmaids had was tipping away from Courtney as she kept adding demands of expensive shoes, specific brands of makeup and colors, and designer jewelry, all of which she expected her bridesmaids to buy so that she would have the wedding of her dreams. So far, the total bill per bridesmaid was exceeding $700 for the "honor" of standing up for Courtney and her groom at their wedding.

"If they love me, they will happily cough it up for me," Courtney rationalized, "because it is *my* special day, after all."

Courtney was deep into her personal bridal pity party as she whined to herself about having such heartless and uncaring friends. The bridesmaids had, in unison, rolled their eyes in spins of disgust at the bouffant hairstyle she had chosen for them to wear and the brilliant shade of crimson red nail polish.

"And I even scheduled the salon appointments for them!" Courtney whimpered defensively. Perhaps it was the memo informing the bridesmaids of the cost of the hairstyle and manicure, for which they were expected to pay, that had turned the perceived mutiny into reality. It was time to take action and whip those bridesmaids into obedience! Gathering them together, Courtney summoned up her reserves of tears and let forth a torrent of sobs.

"It's my special day, and you are all ruining my dreams, my hopes, my vision of my perfect wedding day! This is what I have dreamed of my bridesmaids looking like since I was five years old."

Courtney's manipulative tactics were working. She could see the doubt and confusion flitting across their faces because she knew that it was not in the nature of women to want to be accused of ruining someone else's wedding. Courtney went

On the day of the wedding, the already multi-married bride sent the fifteen groomsmen to a supply store to buy plywood for her walkway. It didn't matter that it was raining cats and dogs; she was going ahead with plans to have this wedding– complete with thirty-five attendants –outdoors.

for the kill: "And if you all loved me, you would want to see me happy and make this the most perfect wedding ever."

That was the coup de grace, and every bridesmaid caved in and sublimated her preferences to Courtney's. With her troops now obeying her wishes, Courtney was free to devote more time to ordering the groomsmen into decorating the getaway car according to her carefully planned designs.

> Briana decided the entire bridal party _had_ to be with her every Saturday to shop for this and that for the wedding. While on a Saturday mission for the bridesmaids' dresses, Briana really showed her vile character deficits. She _hated_ absolutely everything and threw hissy fits in the dressing areas. She would pick out the UGLIEST dresses that were also the most expensive. She just couldn't make up her mind as to color or style. She wasted one store manager's time by promising ever-so-nicely to return and buy dresses if the shop opened up for her the next day, which was Sunday, a day they were normally closed. The store manager agreed. Of course, Briana had no intention of returning.

This is a classic case of Bridezillaism. Here we have a bride who assumed that people are at her complete disposal, much like a paper towel, and are hers to command just because she's got a ring and a date. If anything, a bride should be even more aware of her behavior because she is in something of a spotlight. No one wants to be around a bride who uses and abuses people. We get numerous letters from bridesmaids who want to know how to bow out of a wedding gracefully because the bride, their friend, has turned into an unbearable, demanding, selfish beast. Brides must realize that they are not the center of the universe and that vendors and friends alike are not royal subjects.

When I was asked to be a bridesmaid at my dad's youngest stepdaughter's wedding, it was quite a surprise because I barely knew the girl. I had only met her once—at my father's wedding to her mother. Then when I learned I was going to be her maid of honor, I asked why not her best friend? The bride replied, "She's not pretty enough..."

Why is it that brides think that the wedding party must be made up of physically beautiful people? Attendants should be chosen for the beauty within and their relationship with the bride. Any other reason is simply not acceptable.

My cousin Trina was asked to be the maid of honor at a friend's wedding. After Trina had purchased her maid of honor gown and organized the bridal shower, the bride told Trina that she was no longer going to be the maid of honor because the bride's older sister and mother thought Trina was too fat to be in the wedding.

Clearly this bride is a child. She's still taking orders from her mother, who acts as the Bridezilla on behalf of her daughter. But both have forgotten that friendship is not based on scales of weight, but on scales of kindness and thoughtfulness.

A woman I thought to be a dear friend was getting married. She didn't ask me to be a bridesmaid, which seemed odd, but I just figured that she had lots of family she had to ask. She asked me to be an "honor attendant" to help her in her wedding preparations, since her maid of honor (her sister) lived out of town. Because I thought she was a close friend, I said yes.

She ended up picking five bridesmaids and a maid of honor—four were family members; two were what I can only call passing acquaintances. I was baffled at this selection, but I kept it to myself. As time went on, I noticed something that I include here only because it is crucial to the story of this Bridezilla—all six of the bridesmaids were _very_ overweight. I would say that the least overweight of the six was about 50 pounds overweight, and the heaviest probably weighed around 375 pounds.

The bride was able to coordinate schedules so that all six bridesmaids could be in town on the same day to have dress fittings. I went with her as her "honor attendant" to help see that things went smoothly and to take notes.

When the bridesmaids saw the dress she had picked out for them, they were shocked into silence. When they tried their dresses on, three of the bridesmaids were in tears and trembling in embarrassment. The bride had selected skin-tight, strapless sheath dresses. Now, even though they were all very large women, all of the women were actually quite beautiful. They would have looked gorgeous and felt good about themselves in a different style of dress. But a skin-tight sheath? Every bulge and dimple showed prominently. And strapless? I don't know of any large woman who is comfortable in a dress with exposed arms.

The bridesmaids tearfully asked her to reconsider this dress decision. But the bride went into a conniption fit and said that this was the <u>only</u> dress that fit into the life-long dream she had of her wedding. So they asked if they could order the matching shoulder wraps so that they didn't feel quite so exposed. She continued her fit, ending by whining and producing crocodile tears saying that they were trying to destroy her special day and that if they were good friends and relatives they would just "shut the hell up and wear the dresses she wanted for her day." One bridesmaid had had enough, and told the bride that she quit. Inside I was shouting, "Yeah! You go, girl!" But outside I was still trying to be the calm "honor attendant" and console the sobbing bride.

When we got in the car to leave, Bridezilla revealed herself to be the despicable creature I was beginning to suspect her of being. She said, "It's just awful that Molly quit—the balance of my attendants with his is going to be ruined now!" Gritting my teeth, I offered to step in and take Molly's place. She snorted and said, "You don't get it, do you?" I shook my head in utter confusion. She said slowly and *methodically, as though explaining something to a small child, "You're not fat." Then she went on to explain that she had deliberately picked women who were, "really disgusting and fat." And that she had picked those dresses to highlight their flabby figure so that she would look better. "Next to those oinkers in those dresses with their fat hanging out all over, I am going to look sensational on my wedding day."*

Cruelty is another hallmark of the Bridezilla. While we would never dream of kicking a little puppy, this Bridezilla has no problem mentally thrashing family and friends just so she can insure that she will, by golly, be the focus of all attention on her wedding day. There's faulty reasoning here. Brides are always the focus of attention unless something is dreadfully out of place. A collective group of large women wearing inappropriate attire is sure to be the primary focus of attention, which would then shift to the bride as people come to the horrid realization that she is responsible for a parade of badly dressed, miserable women. It's not about looks, ladies. It's about relationships.

On the other hand...

Two of my good friends were tortured by their evil sister, Queen Mean, when she was married two years ago. My friends are very tall women, 6'1" and 5'11". At the time, one weighed 450 pounds and the other 315. Before the wedding mess, they both thought that they had a close-knit family.

Queenie chose eight bridesmaids to be in her wedding party, none of whom were her sisters. In fact, all of the attendants were relatively new acquaintances, and all were beautiful and thin. When her sisters offered to help with the wedding in any way they could, Queenie told them that if they were willing to lose enough weight to fit into size 8 dresses then they could be in her wedding party. Otherwise, they would just be useful taking care of setup and other "behind the scenes" details. The bride explained, "I will have these wedding photos for the rest of my life. I want everything about them to be beautiful and perfect."

If all the bride wants is an album of photos of herself surrounded by good-looking people, why bother with all the details of a wedding? Surely a photo session with hired models would be cheaper and easier to arrange. Or with digital photography and a little cut-and-paste, one need not bother at all with real people.

The bride had fashion design school aspirations, so she announced she would "design" our gowns and the mother of the bride would sew them. We only had to pay for the fabric and shoes. When we received the bill for the fabric we were taken aback at the excessive cost, but the mother of the bride stated that it was high quality, by a well-known designer. We divided the bill by seven and said no more. The fitting of the gowns required several trips to the mother of the bride's home, and she seemed irritated by the intrusions. She also complained, each time, how much larger my co-worker and I were than the bride (a petite size

4). "You're so big!" she would exclaim with exasperation. Hardly an ego booster. The dresses themselves were beyond hideous. The black, much touted fabric was sateen and covered with small roses. This was to form the overskirt and bodice. The underskirt and huge puffy sleeves were sewn from pink and white striped bed sheets—yes, bed sheets, which we also had to pay for. We grinned and bore it, since bad bridesmaids dresses are practically a tradition.

We dutifully threw her a shower—a lingerie shower that she had specifically requested—paid for cake, appetizers, champagne, the works. I awaited news of the bachelorette party in vain. At the rehearsal, the day before the wedding, another bridesmaid whispered I hadn't been invited to the bachelorette party as the bride wanted to indulge in some questionable activities and knew I wouldn't approve. The dinner after the rehearsal was "pay your own way," so I passed.

The day of the wedding dawned. Crystal and I, as instructed, showed up at the hairdresser's that afternoon. The hairdresser, Philippe, waited, expensive hair extension in hand, which the bride had ordered and failed to pay for. She was a no show, leaving us to deal with the angry Philippe. He took his revenge by putting our hair into beehive upsweeps. Think Martha Washington on a bad day.

It was too late to turn back now. We arrived at the church. Our gifts were cheesy ceramic rose earrings (to match the dress, but nothing else on this earth) and a black ribbon we were instructed to tie around our necks. I was *embarrassed to have my photo taken in this get-up. The bride's uncle was a florist, so the church looked incredible, and the ceremony went off without a hitch.*

Crystal and I drove to the ritzy hotel where the reception was being held. We entered through a magnificent bower of flowers only to stop dead and gasp. The entire room, tables, curtains, flower vases—even the buffet tables—had been swathed in the material used for our dresses! We had financed their decor! Needless to say, we left as soon as possible.

Tacky doesn't even begin to describe the methodical and heinous way the bride and her family treated these bridesmaids. Bridezillaism is not limited to the brides, and here is the perfect example of the mother taking on the role as well. Bridesmaids are supposed to be cherished friends of the bride. Ripping them off monetarily, making snotty remarks, and dressing them up in pseudo funeral garb is bad enough. But the actions of the bride herself—leaving them at the hairdresser's, inviting some to the bachelorette party and others not at all—is testament to the character of this Bridezilla. But the real hallmark of Bridezillaism comes by way of the fanaticism of matching the décor to the bridesmaids' dresses. Can you say "obsessive?"

When my best friend announced she wanted me to be her maid of honor, I was thrilled. I gave her an engagement party at my apartment even though I was on a tight budget.

When the time came to select bridesmaids' dresses, she chose one that cost $225. I said that was more than our pre-determined budget of $185. She replied, "Are you sure you are capable of being the maid of honor in my wedding?" As if my ability to pay for the dress had anything to do with how happy I was for her! I was insulted.

A few weeks later, I was at her mother's house and saw a wrapped gift on a table. I asked what it was for. Her mother said it was an engagement present for Bridezilla and that it hadn't been opened yet because she was saving it for the shower which was taking place four months later. This was because she didn't think Bridezilla would have enough gifts to open at the shower. Did she really think her bridesmaids were intentionally going to host a lame shower?? The shower guest list Bridezilla gave me had forty names. Twelve of them lived out of the country but were included because "They might want to give me a gift."

Throughout Bridezilla's six-month engagement, she made greedy demands of me: she demanded I stay overnight the night before the wedding and the night of the wedding, and she made suggestions about what I should do for her in the way of gifts. She even managed to find out about the surprise bachelorette party and tried to arrange all the little details such as location, transportation, and apparel.

Bridezilla's mother, who was kept informed about the shower plans, called me the day before the shower and launched into me saying, "What the f#*% is wrong with you? You can't have my daughter's shower in a Chinese *restaurant!! It's not good enough. It's not GOOD ENOUGH!!" Well, the shower was beautiful, the food was great, and we bridesmaids picked up the tab for all those attending. The bride's mother never apologized for her outburst.*

On the day of the wedding, about an hour before the conclusion of the reception, the mother of Bridezilla introduced me to some of her friends. "Have you met our rude maid of honor, April? Oh yes, this is our rude maid of honor." I was shocked. I went to the table where my family was and began crying. They said, "We're outta here. You've taken this family's crap too long."

So red-eyed and trying to hide my humiliation, I quietly told Bridezilla that we were leaving without telling her the reason why. I didn't want to be blamed for ruining her wedding day by telling her that her mother was a monster. The next day I called to explain, and she yelled at me. Then her mother called and berated me, finishing off with, "You're not going to get away with this!" After Bridezilla returned from her honeymoon two weeks later, she sent me an e-mail telling me to never contact her again.

The Momzilla has spawned! The Momzilla has spawned!

Pity the poor Bridezilla in this story who is only behaving in a manner to which she was born and bred. Throughout her brief life, Momzilla has catered to her princess's every desire in the mistaken belief that this will make her a superior person. Instead, what gets inculcated into nascent Bridezillas is a serious character flaw which filters life situations and relationships through a "How does this work to my advantage?" screen. Like a common reptile destined to live its life eating only flies while basking on the pond's only lilypad, second generation Bridezillas almost cannot help being what they are because of genetic hardwiring that predisposes them to see the world as owing them.

While some daughters recognize their mother's faults and are determined to go through life without repeating history, this Bridezilla seems quite content to follow in mommy's footsteps and to let mommy berate Bridezilla's friends on her behalf. While we think a mother should be supportive of her children, this is the kind of support that should have been snipped along with the umbilical cord.

Two hours into the reception, the maid of honor came over and grabbed my husband and me and asked us to help her count all the money the bride and groom received as gifts. I thought that was a bit odd, but we went along with it. We went out to the hall and counted it all up: $675 total (there were fewer than 60 guests). My husband went back to the reception. The maid of honor told me, "It's not enough." Not enough *for what? The bride and groom had not paid any of their vendors and they owed $10,000, and everyone wanted their payments. NOW. The maid of honor told me that she told the bride that if she had the money dance enough people would dance with them and give them enough money to pay for all their expenses. The bride had anticipated that she would have 350 paying guests. I had had budget talks with the bride during the planning phase, but she decided that I didn't know what I was talking about and felt that everyone else should pay for her wedding instead.*

We are trying very hard to compose ourselves. Paying guests? Guests do not pay. Hosts pay for the privilege of entertaining their guests. It's tacky enough to hear stories of cash bar weddings, dollar dance weddings, presentation weddings, and the like, but a wedding is not to be funded by anyone other than the hosts. Period. End of discussion. Go to your room.

Prior to the wedding, a bunch of Brandi's girlfriends wanted to get together and give her a "bachelorette girls' weekend." Our thought was some kind of relaxing weekend out of town or at least a trip to a day spa followed by a nice dinner. However, when the idea of a bachelorette weekend was posed to her, she responded that what she really wanted was for everyone to come over and help her do yard work on the fixer-upper she and her fiancé had just bought. We wanted to think she was joking but knew better, since she's famous for recruiting people to help her do all kinds of work before, during, and after parties she hosts. We told her that she was going to be doing yard work and fix-it chores every weekend for the rest of her life, and this was one weekend she should just relax and try to have fun. The girls who organized the weekend planned lunch at a fun restaurant followed by shopping and a trip to a nail salon for manicures and pedicures. After that everyone was to convene at the bride's house for a pasta dinner and slumber party. Even though the slumber party was to be at the bride's house, the girls who organized the weekend bought, prepared, and cleaned up the house for dinner.

Instead of graciously going along with something nice that her friends wanted to do for her, Brandi spent the first two hours of the lunch refusing to speak to the girls who had planned the party. She only warmed up a little after several margaritas, but she basically sulked through the entire day. At dinnertime, one of her dogs chewed up the PJs of one of the girls who had organized the weekend. Brandi's response was to laugh and tell her that a local department store had PJs on sale that week. There was no apology and no offer to replace the PJs. It should come as no surprise that the girls who organized the weekend never even got a thank-you note for their efforts.

But it *would* come as a surprise to hear that these girls actually went through with this wedding. We'll say it again: getting a ring and a date is not license to order people around, get things done "my way," or be pouty, selfish, ungrateful, or generally boorish.

There's a story going around about a bride who had a bridesmaid unexpectedly drop out of the wedding. Rather than just go on with the remaining bridesmaids, it became her Bridezilla mission to fill the dress. There HAD to be an even number of bridesmaids to groomsmen as far as she was concerned. Her solution was to recruit her preteen male cousin who had soft facial features. He would fit the dress perfectly and no one would know!

Oh, please. The role of bridesmaid belongs to special friends and/or family members. A bridesmaid is not just a dress walking down the aisle. If a bridesmaid drops out—for whatever reason—and there's not another close friend who would be delighted to step in (and not be offended for being asked last), then don't find just anybody. In years to come when one looks over wedding pictures and recalls the wedding day, one doesn't want to cringe over the memory of asking someone who was clearly not a good friend to be in the wedding.

BRIDEZILLA ANTITOXIN

Those helpful quick tips that keep the Bridezilla germs far away.

1. Brides need to remember that their wedding is indeed a special event, so the friends they ask to stand at their side should be special people. Not models, not picture frames, not servants. Friends.

2. You cannot demand that people bow to your whim because it's "my day." If you make an appointment, keep it—or cancel it with advance notice.

3. Unless your friends are the sort who would host a party that's morally objectionable, let them decide what kind of shower or bachelorette party to host. This is a gift to you; be gracious.

4. The corollary to #3 is that no one owes you anything because you're getting married. If your friends are all terribly young and inexperienced, they may not know to throw you a shower. If your friends are old enough to know and don't, then consider the message being sent. Parties given to the bride in her honor are done so because people want to do so. The bride's behavior is directly responsible for the warm desires of others to shower her with parties.

5. Bridesmaids are not Fort Knox. They too are on budgets. Keep that in mind when selecting attire and the accessories. If money is the #1 cause of divorce in married couples, it doesn't take much here to ruin a friendship. Be upfront and honest with the bridesmaids about anticipated costs so they can make an informed decision regarding the affordability of being a bridesmaid.

6. If a friend turns down your request to be a bridesmaid, don't forever banish her out of your life (unless she tells you that she's banishing you out of her life). There is a great responsibility to being a bridesmaid, from time commitments to money commitments to showering you with extra attention. Some friends are just not going to be able to make that kind of commitment. It doesn't mean they don't care for you—quite the contrary! They are doing you a favor by being honest with you.

7. If an attendant has to back out, accept gracefully. If you are blessed with a lot of close, understanding friends, you may ask someone to step in. But if the timing seems awkward, best to let the position go unfilled. Do not ask someone you hardly know to fill out a dress. You're asking friends, not dresses, to be at your side. And yes, it's perfectly proper to have an uneven number of attendants.

8. Say "Thank you." It goes a long way, especially among friends.

6) "I AM QUEEN BRIDEZILLA & I RULE THE EARTH!"

Extreme Bridezillas

CHAPTER SIX

Like tales of the Loch Ness Monster, people tend to believe that Extreme Bridezillas are a figment of the imagination of less-than-enthusiastic wedding attendants and family who create such outlandish fables as retaliation for being forced to dress up in a rented tuxedo or to wear an orange chiffon dress. But the evidence overwhelmingly supports the existence of these once rare creatures, and the stories of woe told by their victims are wrenching proof that the Extreme Bridezilla is a dangerous creature capable of unspeakable acts.

They walked into the house, and Wendy immediately threw her bridesmaid bouquet (plastic, because apparently that was the only way to match this hideous shade of blue) on the floor and started jumping up and down on it. We almost didn't recognize Wendy, who practically grew up in our house, because the bride had insisted everyone wear identical hairstyles, and the one she had chosen was not Wendy's style at all. But when she started screaming, "I will never speak to her again!" we recognized her voice. It seems that, at the reception, the bride and groom had taken the microphone to announce that in order to qualify for a mortgage, they had gotten married at city hall four months earlier. But, as the bride explained, she wanted to have her dream wedding and get her china and silver (or, as she put it, "furnish their house"), so they had decided not to tell anyone until the reception. Everyone knew they were living together before the wedding, but no one, not even the parents, knew about the justice of the peace ceremony. The poor wedding guests traveled great distances only to have it sprung on them that what they had witnessed was not a wedding ceremony but an organized gift grab disguised as a wedding.

We are of the opinion that it is perfectly acceptable to drop one's jaw in disbelief, wait for someone to say "Just kidding!" and then make a quick exit when the "Just kidding" never arrives in these types of scenarios, which are becoming all too common these days.

We implore you not to feed the Bridezilla by attending sham weddings if you happen to be informed of the shamness in advance. Sham Weddings, Show-off Weddings, Because We Didn't Want to Wait Weddings, Because I Didn't Get the Wedding I Wanted Weddings are indeed tasteless. The purpose of a wedding is not to show off or execute instant replay with a different outcome. The purpose of a wedding is not to acquire gifts of china, silver, crystal, and toasters (although they are lovely by-products). The purpose of a wedding is serious business. Albeit a most

After the wedding, the bridal party was assembled for photos. For almost two hours. While the guests waited. One shot was taken of the bridal party, one with the bride and her brothers, eight with the bride and groom. For the remainder of the time (well over an hour), the only photos taken were of the bride–alone.

99

happy occasion, a wedding is not something to mock. For those who feel they didn't get to party enough or spend enough money the first time around, an anniversary party (sans wedding dresses, processionals, and other wedding trappings) is a great way to celebrate married life with family and friends.

My husband and I had both been asked to be in a wedding. I had known the bride for eight years and he had known the groom for about ten. Calli became the biggest Bridezilla in recorded history when she issued her "Rules and Guidelines for My Wedding." Some items on her list included:

1. The groom's grandfather (who was an immigrant and in declining health) had to wear a tuxedo if he wanted to be included in any pictures.

2. Her brother had to get a small, pale mole at his hairline removed or he would not be allowed in any pictures.

3. No one was allowed to cut, color, or change hairstyles without consulting with the bride first. Calli actually called her future mother-in-law a bi*&% for getting her hair trimmed and grey roots covered and not consulting with Calli first. The mother-in-law's minor hair work made her look ten years younger which made Calli jealous.

4. One bridesmaid had a pimple on her cheek and a sun spot on her forehead. Calli gave her $15 two weeks before the wedding and said, "Here's your insurance co-payment; go to my dermatologist and get yourself fixed or you won't be in the pictures."

5. The groom and groomsmen were not to have anything to drink at the rehearsal dinner or before the ceremony other than plain water. At the reception, the groom was only allowed to have one glass of champagne; any more than that and Calli threatened to take the honeymoon cruise tickets and go to the Caribbean with her mother.

6. And finally: She told her sister-in-law, "You will not be allowed to come to my wedding if you get yourself pregnant. I won't have you upstaging me on my special day." Of course, the sister-in-law found out two days before the wedding that she was pregnant. She was too scared to tell anyone until several weeks after the wedding!

This bride was so self-absorbed that she bought a $400 outfit and wore it every time she wasn't working for six weeks; she wanted to be prepared for whatever parties she was sure were going to be held for her. Hee hee, we picked her up for her surprise shower on a Saturday right after work while she was still in her restaurant uniform and smelled like catfish. Surprise!

One has to remember that the Extreme Bridezilla is only half of the engaged couple equation, and her demands may not reflect the interests of the groom. The best course of action in dealing with an obsessed Bridezilla is simply to ignore her and act as dignified as possible. In this instance, neither the bride's brother nor the bridesmaid should have followed through with the bride's directive to seek medical assistance in removing small blemishes but should have merely pocketed the money the Bridezilla was so willing to give them. If a bride throws a fit, the goal is to remain dignified so as to impress upon the bride two things: 1) Fits don't accomplish anything, and 2) Calm and reason will prevail.

Mother-in-law should have been free to change hairstyles as she wanted, and Sister-in-law should have been able to share her happy news of pregnancy without fear of a Bridezilla reaction. Naturally, big news like a pregnancy or engagement of another family member is not shared at the wedding or reception lest the focus of the wedding be sent elsewhere. But there was no reason not to share her news with family members prior to the wedding.

The job of the victims of Bridezilla is to remain levelheaded and reasonable in direct contrast to the unreasonable and outrageous behavior of a Bridezilla. We do not concern ourselves with the notion of "What will Bridezilla think of me if I don't go along!" It doesn't matter what Bridezilla thinks, since she obviously cannot think clearly. Therefore, we do not succumb to a Bridezilla's demands. Remember, etiquette requires us to be gracious, not a doormat.

The bride was a co-worker and a pretty good friend—at least at that time. She was highly educated, very proper, and very classy—or so I thought. Once she got engaged, she became the Bride from Hell. Actually, more like a field marshal. She had nine bridesmaids, and she decided she wanted the gowns handmade. The pattern she selected was absolutely atrocious: pink bustier-type bodice with gigantic leg-of-mutton, black sleeves; a black full skirt; and an enormous bow right on the bust line (and for buxom attendants like me and three others it stuck out like a pair of wings). The bride had at least six showers, and the bridesmaids were invited to and expected to bring a gift to each one. By the time we got close to the wedding date, we were all pretty tired of her and what a phony she was turning out to be, and then we got THE MEMO. In it, we were given orders on where to be from the Thursday morning before the wedding until Sunday afternoon after the wedding, what we should wear at each event (cocktail parties, bride's luncheon, bachelorette party, rehearsal and rehearsal dinner, wedding morning breakfast, wedding day lunch, photo session, wedding, reception, morning-after luncheon), and the coup de grace: "If I did not mention before, please plan on wearing red lipstick and red fingernail polish at the wedding."

Now, there's nothing wrong with that if that's your taste for your fingers and lips, but I don't wear fingernail polish. I don't like it and I never wear it. She knew this. And many of the other bridesmaids had coloring that looked absolutely hideous in red lipstick. I went through the roof and called one of the other bridesmaids to say I was going to pull out. She talked me out of it and indicated that I should just skip painting my nails and that the bride would probably never notice. Plus, the bouquets we were to carry would totally hide our hands, so what difference would it make what color our fingertips were?

Starting at the bride's lunch, the questions from the mother of the bride and the two maids of honor (her sisters) began in earnest. "So, do you have your manicure scheduled?" Uh, no. "When are you going to paint your nails?" Uh, when I get around to it. "Why haven't you painted your nails yet?" On the day of the wedding at the lunch, one maid of honor came up to me, grabbed my hands and said, "You better get 'em painted." I told her they were my hands and I would do as I pleased with them, thank you very much. Up until that point I had been thinking about just painting them to be nice, but that little display cemented my resolve not to give in.

When I arrived at the church to dress for the wedding, the Bride from Hell was already there and saw me. The first thing she said to me was, "Show me your hands." None of the usual, "I'm so excited," or "I'm so nervous." Not even a lousy, "Hi, how are you?" was uttered from someone who was my friend. I held out my hands. She said, "I brought red nail polish, and you WILL have red nails in the wedding." I told her, "I haven't painted my *nails in over ten years, and I am not about to start now. You want 'em red, you paint 'em." She had two of the other bridesmaids hold down my hands and paint my nails. I so wanted to walk out, but then I knew she would make me out to be the bad guy. I had never been so furious in my entire life. We never were friends much after that. And, of course, the marriage was over less than two years later. Her ex-husband told me that she was obnoxious to everyone during the entire wedding planning, from caterers to the limo service and everybody else. Seems she had this fairy-tale wedding in mind that she wanted to have and that was what was important, not the ceremony itself or the commitment she was making.*

Blood makes a lovely shade of red for fingernail polish, don't you think? It would not surprise any of us if this story had ended with the bridesmaid walking out. After all, one can only handle so much indignation for the sake of a supposed friendship. Obviously, the advice simply to ignore the demands of the Bridezilla did not work in this case, because the bride did notice and did take invasive action to get her demands met. The bridesmaid grudgingly tolerated this invasion of her body because she feared being made out to be the "bad guy" who ruined the wedding. While this is sometimes a legitimate fear, one must remember that the Bridezilla who dreams of the Perfect Day and takes great pains to insure it is perfect is not likely to stomp down the aisle screaming, "Betsy won't paint her nails!" And those who would listen to her tale of woe would most assuredly wonder how a set of unpainted nails could ruin a wedding unless the bride was—

gasp!—a Bridezilla. Claims of ruining a wedding for changing a hairstyle, becoming pregnant, or refusing to wear red nail polish are ridiculous and should be ignored.

The bride coerced me into letting the small wedding party stop by my one-bedroom apartment for a brief respite in between the wedding and reception. Unfortunately, word spread that my apartment was the place for lunch, and I suddenly faced 140 hungry people and a very angry mother of the bride for being "ill-equipped." Then the bride actually called after the honeymoon wanting to know where my gift was and why she hadn't received it.

As the end of the story relates, virtually everyone knew this bride to be a first-class bullying Bridezilla, but no one effectively stood up to her. This Bridezilla eventually got exactly what one could expect: lost friendships, a divorce, the enmity of her community, little regard, and a spot in the Etiquette Hell Hall of Infamy. We encourage bridesmaids in such predicaments to choose the high road in their ethics and dignity and simply refuse to stand in alliance with Bridezillas who abuse people. After all, one is known by the company one keeps.

The first thing to get my attention was the wedding invitation. It had a detailed menu of the wedding meal along with a request to mail a check for the cost of our meal and drinks when we sent the RSVP. The bride promised that it did not apply to members of the wedding party so I was off the hook. Once at the reception hall, I slipped in the back door of the dining area to drop off my card with a gift of money enclosed and to place the ring pillow and the bride's bouquet at the guest book table. On my way back to the foyer, I noticed a long list of names taped to the door. It was the complete guest list with notations of who had paid for their meal and who hadn't. By the door was a table with a padlocked cash box. The bride intended to collect money from her guests to pay for her reception before allowing them to enter the reception hall!

Translation of the invitation: "I want a grandiose wedding that I cannot afford, so you, my beloved family and friends, shall foot the bill for my dreams." To our horror, this bride is presumptuous not only about her guests' wealth but also about their integrity, such that she has to screen the guests before they enter the reception to shake them down for the required cash for her dream wedding.

It is perfectly acceptable for guests simply to decline this "invitation" or perform a perfectly executed 180-degree turn from the reception entrance and find a more appealing place to dine—like a nice restaurant or home.

A few years ago I was asked to be a bridesmaid and soloist at a friend's wedding. Though we had somewhat drifted apart when I was away at college, we were still friends, and I was at first honored to be a part of Sara's special day.

Sara decided to have the bridesmaids' dresses made by a seamstress, and she was very proud of the fact that the dresses were only going to cost $50. Now, forgive me if I sound mean, but $50 just didn't sound like it would buy fabric that would hold up. Nevertheless, Sara's a take-charge person, so I figured she knew what she was doing, and I surely didn't mind that it wasn't going to dent my pocketbook too badly. So we went to the first fitting—it was at a bowling alley, which sort of made me nervous. The fabric was this cheap-looking, polyester-type fabric (the wedding was in mid-June—HOT) in a medium purple color. So here we all were, thinking that's the color of the dress. No. Since she couldn't find one color of fabric that matched the idea in her head perfectly, she got this odd-looking blue chiffon to go over it. Blended with the purplish polyester, it was a very strange color. When we got to our second fitting, to no great surprise, none of the dresses fitted properly, which would have been fine had the zippers not already been sewn in. That pretty much insured that the dresses weren't going to fit at all unless we all crash-dieted until the wedding, a mere three weeks away. Also, the dresses had a sweetheart neckline, which is not what she wanted, and the sleeves were these crazy-looking, bunched-up, lop-sided balls on either side. They were supposed to be on the shoulder, not off, and the dresses were supposed to be floor-length, not tea, like two of ours were. Yes, some were long and some were short; we didn't know why. Sara seemed to think that three weeks was enough time to fix the problems with all the dresses.

Two days before the wedding, Sara called me, practically hysterical, and said that the hall where her reception was located hadn't told her that staff there would not decorate prior to the reception, so would my fiancé help set up that day? He agreed, figuring that since the wedding was across town and I would have to be at the church early that day anyway, he could help out while I was preparing for the wedding. She also assured him that there would be many others helping out, so he could relax once they were finished and still have plenty of time before the ceremony.

The day of the wedding I dropped off my fiancé at the hall, and I went to pick up my dress. Little did I know the horror that awaited. When I first looked at the dress, I was shocked. This couldn't be right, I thought. The dress was hanging lopsided on the hanger, and the seamstress had flipped the bottom half over the bottom part of the hanger so it was completely wrinkled. The hem of the dress had been taken up even more than before; it was now barely below my knees, and it was longer in the back than the front. On top of that, the seamstress had ripped out the zipper and had taken it in even more. Then she had used white thread to sew the zipper in; threads were hanging out of the seam. She had used black thread to "fix" the sleeves; threads and elastic were hanging out everywhere. I tried on the dress and couldn't breathe. It was horrible and looked worse on. I looked around. We all looked like freaks, except Sara, who looked shocked but nevertheless regained her composure and told us we looked great. I was thirsty and hot, so I got some water from the cooler in the bride's room. The condensation on the outside of the bottle dripped on my dress and stained it. Sara then screamed at me that

I was an idiot and was trying to make sure my own upcoming wedding "upstaged" hers. I was so annoyed at that point, but it was her wedding day so I just tried to cover it up the best I could with the tacky, plastic-looking fake bouquets we were given.

During the ceremony I went to the microphone to sing. I won't even say the name of the song, by the way; it's such a horrible idea for a wedding song that no one in her right mind would use it—except for Sara and her groom. Let's just say that the word "razor" is prevalent in the lyrics. I was humiliated singing it, not to mention the fact that I couldn't get a decent breath since I was sucking in my stomach so much due to the horrible dress I had to wear.

After the wedding, the bride and groom and wedding party piled into the limos they had rented. We headed out to the bars in town. I was hoping that we were going right to the reception because I think it's rude to make people wait at the reception when they've traveled a long way, and my fiancé was waiting for me as well. But in the limo there was an abundance of hard liquor and champagne. Soon almost everyone, except me, was drunk. While we were hanging out at a lame bar, I checked the time and noticed that it was almost time for us to have dinner at the reception. I told this to Sara (who appeared to be drunk), and she glared at me and then made some rude comment about me to everyone in the bar about how I was again trying to ruin her day, but she relented and we went to the reception. Once there, my fiancé ran up to me and informed me that there were only two people decorating the entire hall that day; only he and Sara's old roommate were there, not the scores of people that she had promised. He hadn't even finished with the decorations until about 2:30, and the wedding was at 3:00. He had spent more than five hours decorating, and he was very upset that he had been lied to for Sara's benefit.

Now, for the clincher—dinner. Since this was a typical dance hall, it came with typical inexpensive hall fare—corn on the cob, baked chicken, peas, and mashed potatoes. Not what you'd see at every wedding, but I knew that Sara and her groom didn't have a whole lot of money and they wanted a "party hall" kind of atmosphere, complete with guests serving their own drinks. Anyway, after the head table had gone up to get their food, the rest of the tables got up to get in line for the food too. Then Sara rushed up to me and told me to ask my fiancé to sit down. When I jokingly asked her why, she told me that they had two lists of guests—a "primary" list and a "reserve" list. Apparently, my fiancé was on the "reserve" list! Once the people on the "primary" list ate she would see if there was enough left, then start allowing people on the "reserve" list to eat! I could not believe what I was hearing. First of all, it was absolutely shocking to me that someone could make lists to decide who could and could not eat when they were invited to the reception! Second of all, how dare she say that to me, and to him when he had slaved all morning to decorate for her reception!

At this point my fiancé was very angry and was ready to leave. I promised him that he could have some of my food since he hadn't eaten all day, but Sara said that I needed to eat it, since I would have to keep my strength up for clean-up! WHAT? Yes, after this nightmare of a wedding ended, she made all of her bridesmaids and their dates or husbands clean up the hall! I honestly couldn't believe it. It was gross—cigarettes in plastic beer cups, confetti everywhere, etc. By the time we got back to the hotel (yes, even though we could have gone home, Sara had insisted that we get a hotel room nearby since the bridal party was REQUIRED to attend the gift opening at the hotel the next day...ugh!), it was almost 3:00 a.m. and my fiancé wanted to forget that Sara ever existed.

The next morning we trudged down to one of the tiny conference rooms in the hotel, where the gift opening was taking place. I figured, "Well, we'll just sit here for an hour or two, then go home and get some sleep." Wrong! When we got there, Sara looked at us with a glare and snapped, "You're late! Everyone's tired and wants to get some rest, but we had to wait for YOU to get here before we could start!" I was stunned, but I sat down. Her irritating mother then started passing around huge warehouse-sized plastic containers. I was curious to see what they were— some kind of game, perhaps? When the containers got to me, I came to the nauseating realization that they held the leftover food from the night before, congealed and cold. Lumpy, cold mashed potatoes in a huge bottle. Slimy green peas in a gargantuan tub. Her mom was shaking the "stuff" out on people's plates, and it was absolutely disgusting. When I said I didn't care for any, she mocked me in *front of everyone. We were ready to get out of there. Just when we didn't think we could take it any longer, Sara and hubby FINALLY finished opening gifts—only to start opening the cards! They opened each card, announced who it was from, and said how much money was inside! I was so embarrassed for everyone who gave them cash. Some people looked like they were going to sink into the floor. Her mother, meanwhile, glared at those who were there who had given less than an "acceptable" amount. It was awful.*

Where does one begin to comment in this tale of abuse?

We can understand a bad bridesmaid's dress. It's so common that a perfect dress is what's unusual. We can understand an emergency, such as finding out at the last minute that the hall wouldn't decorate (although we do suggest that these types of emergencies can easily be avoided). But at what point would we have counseled the bridesmaid to say "enough?" That would have to have been when she discovered the two dinner lists at the reception. Staying gave the impression that she endorsed the practice. In case that wasn't motivation enough, then being told at the last minute that she was required to clean up would

The bride and groom had time to kill between the wedding and reception, so they decided to go for a spin in the limo. They got the fun idea to parade around a home improvement store in their wedding garb, stopping in the plumbing aisle long enough for the bride to have her picture taken while sitting on a commode.

have been the moment to leave. It's one thing to ask people to stay and help. It's quite another to demand that they do. We'll say it again: Etiquette requires one to be gracious, not a doormat.

Lauren and my brother Trevor had been living together for six years when they decided to tie the knot with a grandiose white wedding. Lauren had been planning a wedding for three years, wallowing in wedding etiquette and wedding "how-to" books. It's a shame that the advice she had read didn't rub off! She labored under the delusion that every member of our family was fascinated by every facet of her wedding plans, and she frequently sent other family members, including my mother (her prospective mother-in-law) photocopies of progress reports that she sent to her mother, detailing her wants, wishes, plans, and preparations for the wedding.

One of her interests was keeping costs to a minimum, and this was much of the content of these progress reports. I was visiting my mother when one of these lengthy missives arrived from the bride-to-be, and we were both surprised to find a section of paragraphs carelessly scratched out. What we had, in essence, was a photocopied letter to her mother with a portion struck through with a couple of pencil marks but still clearly readable. The portion that had been "scratched out" detailed her intentions for her bridal attendants. She wanted eight bridesmaids, and though she was having trouble coming up with that number among her friends, she was not going to ask me, the sister and only sibling of the groom, to be in the bridal party, even though her brother was to be one of the male attendants. Her reason? She stated that I was "too tall, fat, and unsightly" to fit in with her other wedding attendants! The scratched-out paragraphs went on to state that this decision to exclude me from the bridal party was going to create a "sticky situation," but she "couldn't endure the thought that I would stand in the wedding," so her solution was to ask me to sing instead. She went on to say that I had a "passable voice" and was "somewhat musical," so my performance "shouldn't be too painful." Note that I'm a professional musician with a classically trained voice, and for many years I made my living largely from singing at weddings and other functions. She went on to add that it would save money to have me sing, rather than having to hire a local soloist, so my "musical imperfections could be overlooked in the interest of saving money and keeping the bridal party looking good." (These are direct quotes from her letter!)

Well, to say that I was shocked and then heartbroken is an understatement. I couldn't believe the smallness of this woman—after all, I've seen more weddings than most, and many of them have included family members as attendants, though they might be in wheelchairs, have facial deformities, be mentally handicapped, etc. To have been effectively cut out of my only sibling's wedding for such a reason—yes, I am six feet tall, but I wasn't particularly overweight at the time—was shocking. To add insult to injury, the bride's brother was also very tall and overweight, yet he was to be included in the wedding party!

My mother telephoned my brother and told him what the letter had said; he was shocked at first, but he then went on the defensive and said we shouldn't have read the scratched-out portion, though it was clearly legible! After I calmed down over a few days, I decided that rather than create a miserable situation for everyone, I would simply sing at the wedding as asked, hide whatever pain I felt, and wish my brother well. But it didn't end there!

A few weeks after the delivery of the "insult letter," my brother called my husband and said, "One of the guys I wanted to have for an usher can't make it, so would you be an usher at the wedding?" My husband pointed out that we were financially strapped at the time and that he was working a schedule that couldn't be changed. He went on to explain that he would be making a hurried overnight trip to the wedding locale (about 200 miles away), and that would preclude him from being able to participate in the wedding party; he wouldn't be able to devote the time necessary for tuxedo fittings, the stag party, photography sessions, etc. The bride-to-be shouted from somewhere in the background (clearly audible over the phone) that my husband didn't have to worry about attending or performing any of the male attendants' usual gatherings or duties because he was "only being asked to make up numbers, not because he was wanted as an attendant, and that he wouldn't be invited to the rehearsal supper or stag party anyway." My husband was seething with rage at this point, but he held his tongue and declined graciously, and the phone call was ended on a strained but civil note.

As asked, I had sent the bride-to-be a list of songs that I regularly sing at weddings. I pointed out to her that I know most of the traditional and contemporary wedding favorites and would be glad to sing whatever she wished. I received no response to this. I was able to travel to the wedding locale several days ahead of the wedding, with my husband following on the day of the wedding. I met with Trevor and Lauren to discuss what they wanted me to sing, as the bride-to-be had never acknowledged my list of songs.

Everything started out well enough. Trevor requested that I sing a song that was performed at my own wedding, which he had liked a great deal. I agreed and then made a few more suggestions, but Lauren just sat there like a stone; she hadn't said a word since I arrived at their home. Trevor was quite enthusiastic over the two other songs I suggested, and, since Lauren still said nothing, we finalized the song order for the ceremony. Then she suddenly snapped, "I'd prefer it if you kept your singing to a minimum—the less the better!" and flounced out of the room. Embarrassed, Trevor and I quickly decided on the single song he'd requested, to be sung early on while the guests were filing into the church, and he went off to placate his intended.

Well, I sang as requested, took my place as a guest with my just-arrived husband, and watched as the wedding party processed down the aisle. Several female attendants were larger than I, but at that point I could hardly notice because

Lauren processed wearing a traditional white dress with a shiny satin finish, a fitted bodice with a dropped "pointed" waist, a crown, and a face veil—all over a nearly seven-month pregnancy. No wonder she'd been so bundled up when I met with her about the songs and the other times I'd seen her in the days before the wedding! She had insisted on wearing the dress she originally had made before she was pregnant, even though it fit like a sausage skin, was visibly splitting down the side seams, and blatantly emphasized the fact that she was pregnant! I couldn't imagine a less appropriate outfit for an expectant bride, and you could see her very conservative Catholic family members cringing in embarrassment every time the wedding ceremony called for her to turn in profile to the congregation.

The married couple departed on their honeymoon, and our family breathed a sigh of relief that it was finally all over. Apparently, Lauren had not reserved her insults for me alone but had managed to hurt and offend almost everyone in my family.

But it wasn't over. A couple of weeks after the wedding, I received a telephone call from my father (my parents are divorced). He had been unable to attend the wedding as it was far away; he had some health problems and was forbidden by his doctor to travel. He'd sent a written toast *to the couple to be read at the reception (it wasn't) and a wedding gift of fifteen hundred dollars along with his regrets and he followed that generous check with a beautiful set of ceramic plates made to order by a famous artisan in Maine. He'd received an envelope from the town the newly married couple lived in and opened it, assuming it was a thank-you note. Instead it read: "Mr. Spencer: As you did not see fit to attend our wedding, I'm taking this opportunity to inform you that you are still responsible for your traditional share of the wedding expenses. It is customary for the groom's family to pay for the rehearsal dinner and honeymoon. Your complete financial obligation is $1,683.42. There is an itemized bill attached. Lauren." And indeed, there was an itemized bill for the rehearsal dinner, including liquor, and for the weekend the bridal pair spent at a luxury bed-and-breakfast in New Hampshire! Not one word about the fifteen hundred-dollar check, or the plates, or an inquiry as to his health! Needless to say, that was a bill that never got paid.*

While we can attempt to pass off some of Lauren's horrible deeds to hormonal disruptions, we don't often hear of expectant mommies sending bills out to family for their "share" of a party which they didn't even attend. No, this is nothing but a controlling Bridezilla who was clearly not in control.

BRIDEZILLA ANTIBIOTIC

How to deal with the Extreme Bridezilla

1. Do not feed the beast. Sham weddings are just that—shams—and they are not to be encouraged by attendance or by gifts. This is not to say that one cannot celebrate one's marriage, but such a celebration is not done by making a mockery of the wedding and the vows recited there.

2. Never submit to an abusive Bridezilla. You may be setting a standard and example of moral conviction to bridesmaids and other attendants who lack the ability to defend themselves. Remember, no bride would ever think of ruining her own wedding by running down the aisle screaming about a perceived ruination, like clean fingernails.

3. While an ugly bridesmaid's dress may be an affront to your sensibilities, wearing it is not particularly abusive or permanently damaging to your ego. Requiring extravagantly expensive dresses combined with demands of expensive designer shoes, makeup, hairstyles, and other means of extortion in order to participate in the wedding is inconsiderate and borderline abusive. Forcibly changing someone's appearance is assault. Screaming curses, obscenities, and vile accusations to browbeat bridesmaids into submission is abusive. Lying to get something done that the Bridezilla doesn't want to do herself is out of line. At the first sign of anything that's overly obsessive, expensive, or unreasonable, make a polite but firm exit. It can't be said often enough: Etiquette merely requires one to be gracious, not a doormat.

7) GROOMONSTERS & OTHER FREAKS OF NATURE

CHAPTER SEVEN

"Uuurp!" Bradley was mightily pleased with himself. He had consumed vast quantities of liquid libations and prime rib and had even bitten off the heads of a few of his friends on this, his wedding day. He sat picking his teeth as he stretched out on the bar lounge chair to watch the final seconds of the Duke game while his bride stewed in the reception hall.

"Yes, I made out pretty well today!" he thought to himself. Great meal, lots of booze, great party until he had to leave it to watch his beloved Blue Devils play in the ACC finals. "Hehehe," he chuckled to himself, "and all the loot people gave us! I'm sure we made a profit!"

His reveries were interrupted by the wedding coordinator's plea that he cease his viewing of the basketball game and please come cut the cake. Growling to himself at this unnecessary interruption of his enjoyment of his wedding day, Bradley devised a plan. He was all smiles as the photographer and guests took photos of him and his new wife cutting the cake. Bradley was poised to gently feed a piece of cake to his wife when, to her surprise, he shoved it into her face and up her nostrils. As she gasped and sputtered, Bradley smugly thought to himself, "And that's for taking me away from the game!"

Right before the eyes of his bride and guests, Bradley had evolved into the once rarely seen creature—the Groomonster. Beasts of enormous appetite with thoughts only for themselves, Groomonsters are still rarer than Bridezillas but are becoming more numerous as the opportunity for preying on wedding guests to satiate their lust become more obvious to them. They have all the subtlety of a T. Rex walking through a china shop and can be detected miles away. They are not necessarily mated with Bridezillas although a Bridezilla's actions can summon the latent Groomonster genes to overpower all common sense and decency.

"Run, for this is a power greater than all of us combined! Aiyeeeeeeeeeeeeee!"

After the rehearsal dinner, all of the groomsmen took the groom out for one last night of bachelor freedom before getting married; they stayed out ALL night and returned to the hotel the following morning, the day of the wedding. They apparently had hoped that there would be enough time to sleep off all their "bachelor" activities since the wedding was not until the afternoon. But instead, the groom had one killer hangover by the time the wedding started.

During the ceremony the groom passed out once and threw up two times, but still, the wedding went on. Then the groom was not able to make it to the reception, as he had to be taken to the emergency room and given IV fluids because he was so dehydrated from his night of "freedom." The astonished bride managed to retain her composure and went to the reception by herself, danced with her sympathetic uncle, and cut the cake with her new mother-in-law.

The hallmark of both Groomonster and Bridezilla is the rampant selfishness that pervades their actions, thoughts, and decisions.

The groom made a toast to the bride's parents with something a little different: "I'd like to thank my sweet bride's mum and pop for being horny the night she was conceived."

One has to question the intelligence and devotion of a man who would jeopardize what one hopes is a once-in-a-lifetime celebration by getting so intoxicated the night before that it borders on alcohol poisoning. His actions devastated the careful, months-long planning of his "beloved" bride and placed her in an embarrassing situation. Her memories of their wedding day are forever marred by the images of a groom who was there (partially) in body but absent in spirit. And the bride wasn't the only one who suffered at the hands of this Groomonster; he also put his family on public display.

A double pox and extended stay in Etiquette Hell for the groomsmen who perpetrated this crime. They can neither love nor have much respect for their friend or his imminent wife by choosing to execute their party plans on the evening before and on into the morning of the wedding. A little partying is one thing. Partying to this degree is just too much.

I was recently in the wedding of my cousin, and the bride and groom tried to be a frugal as possible (and it showed). When dinner was served we all got plates of the usual stuff that many weddings are known for: boring dry chicken breast, whipped potatoes, and peas and onions. However, the groom was given a different plate. His had rib-eye and lobster on it and the smell wafted throughout the dining area. He just smirked and said since it was HIS wedding day, he deserved to have something special.

It is the height of rudeness to invite friends and family to a celebration in one's honor and then proceed to feed them what the honored ones consider second-class food. Even when the Groomonster's mother fixed a special dinner on the anniversary of his birth for the "birthday boy," everyone ate the same thing. Better to have waited to share a special dinner with his bride later in the evening than to have made it so obvious how little he thought of his guests and how much he thought of himself.

Last year, I was a guest at Audrey and Colin's wedding. Audrey and I were fairly good friends, but I had only met Colin on two occasions during their two-year courtship and now I know why. Trouble was his middle name and the night before the wedding was no exception.

Colin was known to be a very heavy drinker, so Audrey begged him not to get too drunk at any of the pre-wedding parties. But on the night of the rehearsal dinner, he went out with a bunch of the guys and didn't come home until the wee hours of the morning. He wasn't in very good shape either.

Audrey was incensed and threatened to call off the wedding unless he agreed to limit his alcohol consumption to just the champagne for toasts and go into marriage counseling when they got back from their honeymoon.

But on the wedding day, Colin got drunk again. He made a speech at the reception that sounded more like he had just won some big fishing trophy. He didn't mention Audrey or his family or groomsmen at all! Instead he went on and on about all his good pals who showed up for HIS big day.

As the reception was winding down, some of Colin and Audrey's friends started talking about where to go to continue celebrating. It was pretty much decided that they'd go for a late night dinner, but Colin came around and nixed that idea. He wanted to go barhopping. When they told him it was getting too late for that, he went nose-to-nose with a friend and barked at her, "You B*&%#! This is MY WEDDING! We'll do it MY way or you can just leave!!" His face was red from yelling so hard at her. She dissolved into tears and ran out the door.

One has to wonder why Colin was getting married at all. From this story's perspective, it appears his wedding was all about him and his wants. The death knells were ringing for this relationship, but poor Audrey just would not accept that the warning signs were all there. For whatever reasons, she forged on with a wedding while trying to rein in her groom to no avail. It is a sad marriage indeed that begins life with the demand that the couple seek counseling.

Colin and Audrey will eventually wonder why their friends avoid them. Actions have consequences; one cannot abuse people and expect their undying loyalty and friendship in return.

The groom was the world's biggest big football junkie and a lot of his friends were equally enthusiastic about all things sports, but as it happened, the wedding ended up being held the same day as the big college football playoff. The reception was held in a gorgeous ballroom of a nice resort. As the reception went on, the guests started thinning out. And then, there were no men at the reception at all except the groom and bride's father. The coordinator started looking for the vanishing guests when it was time to cut the cake. She found them rather quickly, eyes glued to the big game on the big screen in the resort's lounge.

The bride and her family were none too pleased that so many people were more interested in the game instead of the wedding celebration. The coordinator offered to bring television sets into the reception, but the bride flatly refused to have her reception upstaged by a football game. After the cake cutting, the groom himself sneaked off to the lounge to watch the last few minutes of the game.

The bride was in tears and decided to go home. But the groom had other ideas. Having had a few drinks, he decided that if he couldn't be with his bride on his wedding night, he would phone a hooker. After a long wait, the hooker and her pimp showed up and found him in the lounge. But by then, the groom had sobered up a bit and thought better of his idea. The groom told the hooker that he had changed his mind and to leave, but she wanted to be paid anyway for time and travel. When the groom said he wouldn't pay, the pimp decided to force the issue. The groom was adamant about not paying so he and the pimp ended up in a brawl with fists flying and punches being thrown. The lounge manager called the police and relieved the groom of having to pay for the hooker. He did however, have to pay a fine AFTER spending the night in jail.

While in some areas of the country the fans' devotion to football can be so profound that it borders on a collective religious experience, placing a sports game higher in priority than a once-in-a-lifetime celebration of matrimony is a rather perverse example of not having one's priorities in life properly ordered. This groom's behavior represented the total opposite of an obsessive Bridezilla in that he had given little weight to the uniqueness of his wedding day and would rather plop his gluteus maximus in front of a TV screen than share the day with all his guests and his new wife.

He further compounded his descent into Etiquette Hell by petulantly deciding he deserved a call girl for his wedding night if his wife wouldn't join him in turning the wedding reception into a football party. His every action on his wedding day just reeks of selfish indulgence to the exclusion of everyone else's preferences.

I was reading through the "Gimme Gimme" stories in Etiquette Hell and recalled a brief but memorable incident from when I was a bridal consultant at a large department store in our large city.

While handing brides and grooms a packet of registry cards, it was considered a wise thing to do to let them know (as tactfully as possible) that the registry cards should be placed only in shower invitations and never in the actual wedding invitations. This kept us from getting yelled at by brides who included them in the invitations and then were roundly chastised by family and friends.

One day, while a bride and her mother were in consultation in our office, a bride and groom came to our customer service office in a crowded area of the store and asked for registry cards. Leaving the bride and her mother with their heads over some lists, I ran over to customer service with the cards and quickly gave them the standard little spiel about the invitations, intending to dash right back.

"What?!" exclaimed the groom, loudly. I repeated myself, slightly taken aback.

"No way!" he said loudly, in the middle of a crowd of customers who were turning to look at him.

"Well," his bride said hesitantly, "maybe we shouldn't..."

"NO way!" he exclaimed again. *"We want gifts! We're spending all this money, and we should have gifts to make up for it! All our friends did that, and we will too. If we don't, we may not get as many gifts!"*

By now everyone in the customer service area had turned around to stare, and his bride was looking embarrassed.

"We're putting them in the damned invitations!" he told her, as that sinking-into-the-floor expression started stealing across her face. *"We have to get something back for spending all this money!"*

Registered at
Tres Tacké

One "commendable" quality of most Groomonsters is that they wear their intentions on their sleeves for all to see rather than opting for more discreet gift grubbing. The groom in this story knew that what he intended to do was a grave etiquette faux pas, but he obviously didn't care because his focus was on making his wedding budget balance sheet come out in the black. He took cheapness to new and gutter-level lows, as he wanted the nice party but didn't want the consequence of footing the entire bill to pay for it. Friends and family were merely fiscal/material goods producers he needed to offset his wedding expenses.

The excuse "All our friends did it" is a poor one for following in the footsteps of the etiquette-challenged, who are doomed to rot in Etiquette Hell for their greed. When it comes to following friends in certain habits, greed is not one that is tolerated by one's friends and family. (We shall toss the department store into Etiquette Hell at a later date for even having those ghastly cards. They simply are not acceptable for any use whatsoever!)

At a wedding reception I had the "pleasure" of attending, the couple's parents had arranged for a video slide show of their life from birth to marriage, apparently with a lot of input from the couple. First we watched a half hour of pictures of the groom with his ex-girlfriends. Then it came time to watch the bride's slideshow. We had made it through a few early childhood pictures when the groom suddenly jumped up, shut it off and grabbed the microphone from the bandstand. He proceeded to perform his own medley of Top 40 pop songs and disco oldies, with all the pelvic thrusts, and even jumped on a table. He sang like this for over an hour. And no, he was not singing songs to the bride, which would have been sweet. At the end of this bizarre musical marathon, he announced that he wanted to thank all the MEN in his life for making him the man he was today. He called up to the front everyone from his father to his gardener. Meanwhile, his poor mother and grandmother, who had put it all together, sat in the back and stared in complete disbelief.

No one except one's own mother is interested in a movie version of your life story. And in this case, even the groom's own mother wasn't interested. Guests really shouldn't be held captive to an Elvis-wannabe groom who abuses his very polite audience with

The night before the wedding, the groom and friends were entertained by strippers in THE most intimate way. In the groom's toast at the reception, he remarked, "One of the things I love about my bride is her innocence and acceptance of me. Heck, I could go do a stripper and she would love me still!"

performances of his "talents." Singing one song to the beloved new spouse is sweet indeed; but an hour of karaoke, singing, dancing, and thrusting body parts, supposedly to entertain the guests, could be considered cruel and unusual punishment, especially since the guests committed no crime.

Weddings are not the Academy Awards nor are they a custom episode of "This Is Your Life!" The rehearsal dinner is a more apropos time for some public expression of gratitude to those who influenced the bride's and groom's lives, but even then it should be kept to a minimum lest the attendants begin to question their participation and wonder what they're in for the next day.

We feel rather bad for the groom's father, who was lumped in the acknowledgements by the groom along with the gardener. Either that's a great gardener (and we'd like his number, please) or the groom doesn't understand what it means to express true appreciation for those special people. This is a good time to remind one and all that the wedding is not about you, but you and the love of your life, who, one hopes, is not also you. Toasts should always include mention of the most important person in your life and particularly the fine attributes of the new spouse at your side.

The reception was held at a posh country club with a very nice swimming pool. The banquet room had a nice big balcony that looked out over the golf greens on one side and over the pool on the other. The bride and several members of her family got very drunk, as did the groom. They staggered around the entire evening, talking to people and getting more slurred and bleary-eyed every minute.

Then, as if suddenly inspired by some ape-man movie, the groom ran out onto the second floor balcony, took off all his clothes, screamed and waved his penis at the onlookers, and then jumped off the balcony into the pool. Many of the guests, who were none too sober themselves by this time, proceeded to yell and scream and fling champagne glasses and beer cans into the pool after the groom. Then several guests also stripped down and jumped into the pool and joined the groom in his midnight swim. The bride had a tantrum and left.

Moderation is the key word for this story. Moderation in drink would have led to moderation in behavior. Undoubtedly the groom and friends have by now sobered up and are duly mortified about their behavior, which we hope was not captured on videotape to become fodder for some television wedding blooper show.

Did the bride have a right to throw a tantrum and leave even though she too was toasted? She was in the awkward position of being newly married to the naked diver and thus would have seemed to condone his actions had she stayed and watched or participated as some of the others did. While some parties are very casual, this one was just a bit too casual, so the bride was probably smart to leave lest she herself became the object of a frat house prank. However, a more proper response would have been for her simply to exit the reception quietly with a measure of dignity.

I interviewed a videographer for a newspaper's wedding insert. He offered to show me his "outtakes" tape—snippets of oddities from weddings he had videotaped. The last segment featured the cake cutting at a wedding reception. The bride and groom came together for the routine cutting. Suddenly, the groom grabbed the bride by the neck, hiked himself up on his toes for added thrust, and slam-dunked his bride headfirst into the wedding cake. The impact was so great that the legs at one end of the table collapsed. The bride slid down the table on top of the crumpled cake while faint gasps and cries could be heard in the background.

The bride stood up slowly and turned dramatically toward the camera with arms spread open to exhibit the extent of the damage. Her right side was literally encrusted in wedding cake from head to knee. Her face was smeared with frosting, her hair and headpiece were covered, and cake was falling down the front of her dress. She stood alone for a minute before the groom appeared on the screen, holding his arms out to her in a peace-offering gesture as if to say, "It was just a joke, honey." He reached to embrace her. She turned away from him and exited the reception hall. The videographer said the couple never came to pick up the tape.

We don't like cake smashing. We don't like it one bit. It doesn't speak well of those who participate, as it is a rather juvenile and disrespectful act to smush wedding cake in the new spouse's mouth, hair, face, and/or clothing instead of lovingly feeding it to one another. It is a relatively new phenomenon in which either one or both newlyweds participate in the smash and proceed to smear cake all over the other person's face. We know of one bride who proudly admitted to having a special cake in addition to the wedding cake in order to have an all-out cake fight with her new husband while still dressed in their wedding finery. A variation of the cake smash is when it appears that the bride and groom are about to feed each other a piece of cake but at the last moment move past each other to smash cake in the faces of their unsuspecting best man and maid of honor standing nearby.

The groom passed around copies of his registry in our department at work. Hint taken, the bosses threw a shower and we all gave gifts. Then the groom pinned a wedding invitation to the bulletin board but told us all privately not to show up.

Why are Miss Jeanne and Auntie Noe so vehemently opposed to cake smashing? At what other times in one's life would anyone dream of a public exhibition of food fighting? Using the excuse of a wedding reception shows poor respect for the dignity of the occasion. Most times, only one newlywed is in on the smash and inflicts it on the other as some sort of self-gratifying joke at the other's expense. It is simply a variation of the proverbial pie in the face, meant to insult or show disrespect. A caring, loving person who just took vows to love, honor, and cherish doesn't embarrass his/her new spouse moments after. We also object on the grounds that the guests tend to do nothing but laugh nervously at best because they are embarrassed to witness such childish behavior.

The groom in the story is not just disrespectful but appears to be physically abusive as well. He apparently never considered that his new wife would not find it funny to have her hair, makeup, wedding dress, and wedding cake ruined in front of everyone they knew. We could hazard a guess as to the various psychological meanings behind his actions: either he did not know her as well as he thought, or perhaps he did and knew his act would precipitate an early demise to a marriage he may not have wanted in the first place. In any case, using his height and strength to drive her into the wedding cake, destroying it and the table, was an aggressive act of an honest-to-goodness Groomonster. The bride did the only proper thing she could do, which was silently to leave the reception.

GROOMONSTER ANTITOXIN

Those helpful quick tips that keep the Groomonster
germs far away.

1. Marriage is hard enough as it is without starting off with
an act of public disrespectfulness that humiliates the other
spouse and causes a new barrier to the health and happiness
of your marriage. That means no drunken debaucheries the
night before the wedding, no drunken revelries at the reception, no cake smashing. And—do we also really need to say
this—*no hookers before or after the wedding!*

2. Please save the wedding cake fights for the privacy of your
bedroom on the wedding night. We are not about to tell you
not to smear icing all over each other AFTER you're all alone.
But we do implore a measure of reason and respect when
cutting and eating the cake at the reception.

3. Repeat after us: "I love my wife more than the Super Bowl/
ACC playoff/Stanley Cup/Blue Devils and will honor her with
my devoted presence at our wedding reception no matter how
great the game is predicted to be." Set the VCR and enjoy
it later.

4. Unless you're having a theme reception in which all are
willing to participate, leave the karaoke machine at home
and do not torture your captive audience with renditions of
your favorite songs. Guests come to see you get married, not
perform a Broadway musical.

5. Remember to mention your lovely new bride in your toasts.
In fact, she should be the only major topic of your toasts.

6. Your wedding is not a financial venture in which the person
with the most gifts wins. It is a ceremony to mark the occasion
of taking precious vows to spend the rest of your life with one
special person.

8) YOU SHOULD THANK ME FOR NOT DESTROYING TOKYO!

CHAPTER EIGHT

The simple art of a proper thank-you eludes not only Bridezillas but also most everyone on the face of the planet. It's not difficult to say "thank you" and state why a gift is appreciated, yet people in this "It's all about me!" era are simply stuck on *why* they should say thank you and how to do it. After all, the Bridezilla is just certain that a marriage license is also a license to be given lots of gifts with nary a thought about being grateful.

The reason why one should say thank you is because gift giving is optional, and when one has received a gift, one has been paid a high compliment. Let's repeat this important point: In spite of what one may hear or believe, *gift giving is always optional.* Brides should NOT expect gifts just because they tiptoe down that magical aisle of matrimony. (However, we will flog any guest who attends the wedding and reception and fails to mark the occasion with at least a token gift.) Registries and prodding with "what do you want" queries notwithstanding, each gift is to be treated with surprise, and each guest who gives a gift is to be treated with gracious accord.

My wife and I were invited to the wedding of someone she had met through an association with a charity group. We had become good friends with the bride and her fiancé over the course of a few years, so we gave the couple a rather expensive imported crystal vase as a wedding gift. A few days after the couple returned from their honeymoon, my wife came home from a committee meeting with the vase. Apparently the groom had held the vase up to an ultra-

violet light, and inspected it like he was looking for gold. In doing so, he found a minuscule line in the crystal. The bride gave the vase back to my wife so that we could take it to the store where we had purchased it and get them one that was not "damaged goods."

It's one thing to return a gift to the giver due to malfunction or breakage, but it's an entirely different circumstance to return a gift because it does not meet with one's standards of taste or perfection. The latter reflects a lack of appreciation for the thought that went into the gift and reveals an ungratefulness that is expressed in a critical evaluation of the gift's value. If a gift is defective and one knows where it was purchased, one should call the store and inquire about procedure for replacement. Only involve the donor if the gift arrives broken or if it's absolutely necessary to inquire about the location of purchase in order to correct a problem with an otherwise lovely gift.

While sending a gift to the bride and groom is not a requirement in order to attend the wedding, most guests do send gifts, either because they wouldn't dream of not sending a gift lest they be branded as Neanderthals or because they really want to (lest they themselves be tossed into Etiquette Hell for being unwilling to mark the occasion even minimally). It becomes poor etiquette when there is an expectation of receiving gifts that then mutates into a belief that one can dictate the guests' gift giving. That registries are commonplace and even expected does not mean the bride can dictate the actual gift choice; that choice still lies with the guest. The expectation further manifests itself as disappointment, anger, or petulant rejection of gifts not on the registry or deemed unwanted. One cannot write an effective and sincere thank-you note if the prevailing attitude is one of ungratefulness for what one has received.

Even if the gift does prove to be something completely unidentifiable or horrid, it's incumbent to remember that the guest selected the gift in hopes of pleasing the recipient. Occasionally, there will be a guest who gives something without such noble intent; nonetheless, a proper and polite response is required as it is not the recipient's place to try to determine an intent of anything less than kind.

Here's a sample bare-minimum note that expresses appreciation for that "unusual" gift:

Dear Aunt Marci,

How can we ever thank you for the plastic houseplant? It's a most unusual variety, and neither George nor I can ever recall seeing such a unique item! We appreciate you thinking of us and are looking forward to seeing you next month.

Love,
Gertrude

That's not so difficult, is it? Remember; all gifts are to be received kindly and without expectations. And of course, those notes of thanks are sent immediately upon receipt of a gift.

While dancing with my nephew at his wedding reception, his bride waltzed over to us, smiled ever-so-sweetly, and said, "Hi, Aunt Grace! Where's your envelope?" I didn't have any idea what she was talking about so she started wagging a little white satin purse in my face. It was stuffed with cash and checks and cards. My sister, the mother of the groom, came to the rescue and said, "Aunt Grace sent that big round box that's sitting in our den, remember?" The bride looked like a light bulb went off in her head as she remembered, then said as a way of explaining herself, "Lots of people haven't given us their gifts yet, so I just wanted to make sure they get a chance to see me." And she waggled that purse some more like she really expected me to cough up yet another gift right then and there! Then she waltzed off, swinging her purse, heading for another cluster of guests to give them a "chance to see her." The groom's mother looked like she wanted to die a thousand times.

A few days after a co-worker returned from his honeymoon cruise, I found a little white envelope on my chair. It contained a card with a golden **THANK YOU** *screaming across the front. Inside, the card was completely blank. It wasn't even signed. I later confirmed this was indeed the thank-you note for the office gift and individual wedding gift I had given him and his bride.*

Again, we're dealing with a bride who expects more than she ought. On the one hand, she should have been greeting the guests. On the other, she should have been greeting them so she could visit, albeit briefly, with the dear friends and relatives she had invited to witness the vows and join in the celebration. Dunning them for gifts should have seemed so repugnant that she would never consider such a thing. This Bridezilla carried a mental tally of who gave what and who didn't give—and the tally was not even accurate!

An even stranger notion is the presumption that guests should bring cash to the wedding. The reasons are many: cash bars, dollar dances, "birdcages" and "wishing wells," the presentation... and so on ad nauseam ad Pepto. Guests should feel free to leave their wallets at home. Extortion in any form at a wedding is in exceedingly poor taste.

I sent a college chum a nice card for her wedding and enclosed a fairly generous check for the occasion. Since it had been sent to her the same week I received the wedding invitation, I would have thought a thank-you note would have arrived before the big day. But I never received a thank-you note. When I was reconciling my bank state-ment a couple of months later, the cashed check was enclosed. Upon closer inspection, I noticed she had written "Thanks" in the memo portion.

Horrors! Writing "Thanks" on the check isn't a proper thank-you no matter how one attempts to justify it. A gift of money, while considered improper by some etiquette writers, represents time spent earning it and consideration of how best to please the couple with a gift. A gift of money is the most desired wedding gift these days. Therefore, this most desired gift is surely deserving of a proper and immediate note of thanks. The mere seconds it takes to write "Thanks!" on the check is insincere and oh so tacky.

Several years ago I attended the wedding of one of my clos-est friends from high school. I had made a ceramic water dispenser for her, carefully wrapped it, and put it in a box that originally held a clock-radio. I drew thick lines through the picture clock-radio, expecting her to realize that some-thing different was inside. Ha! The thank-you note I received said, "Thank you so much for the clock-radio. We love the dual alarm feature!"

One can only hazard a guess as to why the box was not opened. Was the bride eager to get out her thank-you notes in a prompt manner? Had someone else been in charge of giving the bride her list of gifts in order to help her write the notes? No matter—the couple should have opened each gift themselves in order to write a proper note. A proper note will make specific mention of the gift as well as of a special quality or its intended use. A note proclaiming nothing more than "Thanks for the radio" or "I love it!" is not sufficient.

My college suitemate decided to get married. We had both majored in journalism, and as her fiancé was a book editor, I decided I would get them a two-set edition of the Oxford English Dictionary (OED). It was rather expensive, but I knew she longed for it and I knew her fiancé would benefit from it also. In the flyleaf of both volumes I wrote a Shakespearean quote on love and signed my name. I received a prompt note of thanks which went on and on about how glad they were to have the set and how much use they'd both get out of it.

Several weeks after the wedding, I was on a business trip and my car over-heated. While waiting for it to be fixed, I decided to kill time in a used bookstore down the street. While browsing the stacks, I happened on a rather new looking OED set. Thinking I might want to get it for myself, I pulled out the books and started flipping through to check for wear. There on the flyleaf, in my handwriting, was the inscription I had written to the bride and groom and my signature! I bought the set—again—and took it home. When I returned from my trip, I called the bride since I hadn't spoken to her in a couple of weeks to see what was new, catch up, and just chat in general. At an opportune time, I asked if they were still enjoying their OED. She said, "Oh, yes! In fact, Bob has been using it on a big project this week!" Later I found out they had sold almost all of their books to pay off some old debts, but in the interim, she had told me they had lost their books due to water damage from a leak in the upstairs apartment. I was so mad about being lied to that I wrapped the OED set and gave it to her on her birthday. You should have seen the look on her face!

At first thought, we want to put the gift giver into the warm place for being rather devious with the bride. After all, she did find out that her gift was not specifically picked out and rejected but that a financial situation necessitated the selling of "most of their books." In the end, however, we agree that the bride borrowed trouble when she proceeded to get creative and state her husband had just used the dictionary. Saying, "The OED was a lovely gift and we so appreciate your thoughtfulness" would have been plenty. It admits nothing about not having the gift in possession and reinforces the donor's thoughtfulness. One need never be specific when such nosey questions are posed; one merely needs to repeat accolades for the thoughtfulness. The other lesson here is that the final disposition of a gift—any gift—is up to the one receiving it. While care must be taken to try to insure the donor never discovers the gift in a used

The bride was given a lovely shower and she received many gifts; however, she failed to send thank-you notes. Then wedding invitations didn't arrive. A week before the wedding, the parents sent a notice saying the wedding was off. It seems the groom's divorce from a previous marriage wasn't final yet. But the bride kept all the gifts just the same and never sent a single thank-you note.

bookstore or church charity sale or—horrors—re-gifted back to the donor in a memory lapse, it still remains the option of the recipient to use a gift in any way he wants, *after* the thank-you note is in the mail.

BRIDEZILLA ANTITOXIN

Those helpful quick tips that keep the Bridezilla germs far away.

1. Thank-you notes are written within two weeks upon receipt of a gift or, if gifts are received at the reception, two weeks upon return from the honeymoon. Some sources, such as magazines, will claim one has three to six months to send a thank-you note. This is simply not true. By then, the guest is thoroughly irritated at not receiving a note of thanks and after waiting that long, the couple might tend to put off writing notes one more day, week, month—until finally a year has passed and the couple wonders why some people won't talk to them anymore.

2. Technically, shower gifts are exempt from thank-you notes because the bride will have gushed her thanks to the guest on the spot. However, it has become very expected by guests that a thank-you note will be written. Therefore, do it. And please, don't ever ask a guest to address his/her own thank-you note envelope. *Très* tacky!

3. Thank-you notes are written on good quality plain paper with black or blue-black ink. You do not need to buy or use special monogrammed stationery. Most important, it is absolutely incorrect to use notes with THANK YOU screaming across the front. Your own words of thanks will be enclosed within.

4. Unless one has a true physical limitation, thank-you notes are always written by hand. If there is a physical condition that makes writing difficult, then typed notes are permissible; one should do one's best to sign the note. Sloppy handwriting does not qualify as a physical limitation. If one's handwriting is terrible, then printing is just fine.

5. Mailing labels are not used for thank-you notes. Write the envelope by hand unless there is a true physical limitation.

6. Thank-you notes are gender friendly; grooms may also write thank-you notes.

7. Notes are signed by one person, but the other is mentioned in the body of the note. For example: "Groom and I were so pleased..." The bride would then sign this note.

8. Never combine a thank-you note with any other type of correspondence. It's beyond tacky to kill two birds with one stone by writing a combination thank-you/birthday greeting or thank-you/Merry Christmas. To be precise, notes of thanks are not included within any other type of correspondence. A thank-you note is a solo note and it flies on its own.

9. Thank-you notes need not be wordy, just reasonably sincere. Each note should be written on its own merit—no writing the exact same note over and over.

10. Thanks should also be sent to people who give the gift of time or effort. People who run errands, help decorate, or offer support are all equally deserving of a note of thanks.

11. If ever in doubt as to whether or not to send a note of thanks, err on the side of caution and send a note. Better to be thought a gracious person than not.

IT'S MY (JUDGMENT) DAY!

EPILOGUE

"What a day!" Courtney mused to herself. She had screamed, cried, cajoled, wheedled, and threatened her wedding party minions and her family into executing a perfect wedding day. But appearances can be deceiving, and as the last pleasant memories of the honeymoon faded like a sunset, Courtney came to realize that all was not well on the homefront. Her new mother-in-law acted cool towards her, her friends all seemed to be busy when she wanted to visit with them, and the invitations to dinner parties dwindled down to nothing. And then, with a growing horror, it dawned on Courtney. She was in Etiquette Hell, cast there by her friends to rot for all eternity. Like a panicked animal, Courtney felt the walls of her social ostracism close in on her like a black, fiery vise. Doomed! Doomed forever!

Or was she? Is there redemption for the repentant Bridezilla?

As we said in the beginning, these are true tales of Bridal Badness. While we giggle and make fun of these women (and men) who provide us with such train-wreck type of amusement, we do not delight in the fact that people actually do these things and behave like this. We want to sit them down in a big comfy chair, put a cup of chamomile tea in their hands, and ask, "WHAT WERE YOU THINKING?!?!" Since we don't run a home for Wayward Bridezillas and because HMOs won't cover a psychiatric admission for a psycho bride, we have taken to other means to warn friends and family and to open the eyes of those who would so readily find themselves in Etiquette Hell.

No one wants to condemn brides to everlasting torment in the bowels of Etiquette Hell. Brides should be all that we want them to be: gracious, kind, and beautiful inside and out. But if plopping one into that extra warm place serves as sufficient warning and turns the heart of a would-be-Bridezilla into all that is charming and lovely, then so be it.

So how does the repentant Bridezilla crawl her way out of the fiery pits of Etiquette Hell and back into the good graces of her friends and family? With a genuine humility that expresses regret for despicable behavior inflicted on those she allegedly loved. A Bridezilla's actions are hers alone in causing the consequences she now endures, so shifting the blame to others or blaming wedding planning stress are not acceptable avenues to exit Etiquette Hell. A face-to-face admission of guilt—and perhaps a little bouquet of flowers—and a plea for forgiveness are best, but barring that, a written note offering a sincere apology is in order.

Dear Betty Bridesmaid,

Now that the wedding has come and gone and I reflect upon being surrounded by dear friends and family, it has dawned on me that my behavior towards you during the wedding was beastly and reprehensible. There was simply no call for me to scream that you were an "idiot" and throw my bouquet at you in front of all the guests at the reception. I am writing in the sincere hope that you can forgive me for my bridal insanity and restore me to one that you would call "friend." I realize this is a great deal to ask after my ill treatment of you, you whose friendship I do cherish; I am deeply ashamed of the injury I inflicted on you and wish to make amends to you if you would be willing.

I'll call next week; perhaps we can get together over lunch?

Most fondly,
Courtney

There is no guarantee that apologizing will repair all the damage done by a Bridezilla, but it's the place to start. Relationships are a very delicate thing. Care must be taken to preserve them, and strong efforts must be extended to repair them when damaged. We can only hope that the friends and family of a Bridezilla are willing to be gracious and accept the olive branch offering when—and if—offered. If the Bridezilla never has the post-wedding awakening of true realization, then family and friends may still offer up forgiveness in their hearts. Do take note, however: the unrepentant Bridezilla quite often carries her boorish behavior with her throughout her life.

To all repentant Bridezillas, we encourage you and support you in your efforts to make amends as best you can. You will find yourselves out of the bowels of Etiquette Hell and living in the warmth of redemption with your sincere attempts to rectify any Bridal Badness.

Miss Jeanne and Auntie Noe really don't want to condemn anyone to Etiquette Hell, yet we find we must when left with no alternative. If you've been exposed to an episode of Bridezillaism or any gross breach of etiquette, tell us about it. Pour your heart out to us. We understand.

www.etiquettehell.com

NOE SPAEMME

Noe Spaemme is the pseudonym for Gail Dunson, a certified etiquette and international protocol consultant. Her background includes twenty years of experience in media and entertainment in addition to being the "Church Lady" for weddings for the past decade. Noe's study of etiquette and protocol came at an early age; it was prerequisite to participate in various activities and to be able to join groups such as the world-renowned Texas Girls' Choir. Her experience in running her own business for high-profile clientele and numerous out-of-the-ordinary life experiences continue to shape her "cut-to-the-chase" approach in helping the countless people who write to her for her practical (and often humorous) advice in navigating tricky etiquette situations as well as everyday protocol issues. Noe and her husband live in Texas.

JEANNE HAMILTON

Jeanne Hamilton's love of information collection, storytelling, and web page administration led earlier to the creation of the uproariously funny yet sobering web site www.etiquettehell.com, the establishment of the moderated email forum EtiquettEmail, and now the writing of this humble volume. Jeanne's experience is the perfect background for this book. Having earned a B.A. in Psychology from Towson State University, she served as a policy analyst and lobbyist on Capitol Hill, that hub of unselfish service and respectful decorum. A wife and mother of three, her experience ranges from being a soccer mom to serving in local civic organizations to coordinating numerous weddings and receptions, both privately and professionally, so Jeanne is well-qualified to identify brats of all kinds, including the bridal variety.

SELECTED BIBLIOGRAPHY & RESOURCES

Gabler, Neal. Life: The Movie - How Entertainment Conquered Reality. New York: Vintage, 1998

Geller, Jaclyn. Here Comes the Bride. New York. Four Walls Eight Windows, 2001

Lichter, Linda S. The Benevolence of Manners. New York. Regan Books, 1998

Kasson, John F. Rudeness & Civility. New York. Hill and Wang, 1990

Barson, Michael and Steven Heller. Wedding Bell Blues. San Francisco. Chronicle Books, 2000

"Many Eminent Writers." Social Abominations. Harrisburg. E.K. Meyers, 1892

Wells, Richard A. Manners Culture and Dress. Springfield. King, Richardson & Co., 1891

Caldwell, Mark. A Short History of Rudeness. New York. Picador, 1999

U.S. Census Bureau

Bureau of Labor Statistics

ACKNOWLEDGEMENTS

With many thanks to those who have been so supportive and offered encouragement during this process: my beloved husband, Candace Laurie, David Feldman, Bob Dauber, Stephen White, Deb McG, and the Belles: Anne, Bev, Jami, Kathy, Lisa, Marti, Rosemary, and Sue. I thank God for His grace and tender mercies.

- Noe Spaemme

With grateful thanks to my patient children, to Anita Letkemann and Michael Violette, and to Phil Sasser who appreciates the irony. With adoring gratitude to my wise husband and awed thanksgiving to God in Whom there are no coincidences.

- Jeanne Hamilton

The authors send their extra special thanks to all the fans of www.etiquettehell.com who contributed their own tales of wedding woes. Without you, there would be no Etiquette Hell and no Bridezilla: True Tales from Etiquette Hell.